21ST CENTURY BREAKDOWN

CD Art Courtesy of Warner Bros. Records/WEA Corp.
CD Art Design, Photography & Stencils: Chris Bilheimer
Back Cover Photo: Marina Chavez
Cover Inspired by Sixten

Alfred Music Publishing Co., Inc.
16320 Roscoe Blvd., Suite 100
P.O. Box 10003
Van Nuys, CA 91410-0003
alfred.com

SING US A SONG OF THE CENTURY

THAT'S LOUDER THAN BOMBS
AND ETERNITY
THE ERA OF STATIC AND CONTRABAND
THAT'S LEADING US TO THE PROMISED LAND
TELL US A STORY THAT'S BY CANDLELIGHT
WAGING A WAR AND LOSING THE FIGHT

THEY'RE PLAYING THE SONG OF THE CENTURY
OF PANIC AND PROMISE AND PROSPERITY

TELL ME A STORY INTO THAT GOODNIGHT

SING US A SONG FOR ME

21ST CENTURY BREAKDOWN

BORN INTO NIXON I WAS RAISED IN HELL
A WELFARE CHILD
WHERE THE TEAMSTERS DWELLED
THE LAST ONE BORN,
THE FIRST ONE TO RUN
MY TOWN WAS BLIND FROM REFINERY SUN

MY GENERATION IS ZERO
I NEVER MADE IT
AS A WORKING CLASS HERO

21ST CENTURY BREAKDOWN
I ONCE WAS LOST BUT NEVER WAS FOUND
I THINK I AM LOSING
WHAT'S LEFT OF MY MIND
TO THE 20TH CENTURY DEADLINE

I WAS MADE OF POISON AND BLOOD

CONDEMNATION IS WHAT I UNDERSTOOD

VIDEOGAMES OF THE TOWER'S FALL
HOMELAND SECURITY
COULD KILL US ALL

WE ARE THE CLASS OF 13
BORN IN THE ERA OF HUMILITY
WE ARE THE DESPERATE IN THE DECLINE
RAISED BY THE BASTARDS OF 1969

MY NAME IS NO ONE
THE LONG LOST SON
BORN ON THE 4TH OF JULY
RAISED IN AN ERA OF HEROS AND CONS

THAT LEFT ME FOR DEAD OR ALIVE

I AM A NATION
A WORKER OF PRIDE
MY DEBT TO THE STATUS QUO

THE SCARS ON MY HANDS
AND THE MEANS TO AN END
IS ALL THAT I HAVE TO SHOW

I SWALLOWED MY PRIDE
AND I CHOKED ON MY FAITH
I'VE GIVEN MY HEART AND MY SOUL
I'VE BROKEN MY FINGERS
AND LIED THROUGH MY TEETH
THE PILLAR OF DAMAGE CONTROL

I'VE BEEN TO THE EDGE
AND I'VE THROWN THE BOUQUET
OF FLOWERS LEFT OVER THE GRAVE
I SAT IN THE WAITING ROOM
WASTING MY TIME
AND WAITING FOR JUDGEMENT DAY

I PRAISE LIBERTY
THE "FREEDOM TO OBEY"
IS THE SONG THAT STRANGLES ME.
DON'T CROSS THE LINE

DREAM, AMERICA DREAM,
I CAN'T EVEN SLEEP
FROM THE LIGHT'S EARLY DAWN

SCREAM, AMERICA SCREAM
BELIEVE WHAT YOU SEE
FROM HEROS AND CONS?

KNOW YOUR ENEMY

DO YOU KNOW THE ENEMY
DO YOU KNOW YOUR ENEMY
WELL, GOTTA KNOW THE ENEMY

VIOLENCE IS AN ENERGY
AGAINST THE ENEMY
VIOLENCE IS AN ENERGY

BRINGING ON THE FURY THE CHOIR INFANTRY
REVOLT AGAINST THE HONOR TO OBEY

OVERTHROW THE EFFIGY
THE VAST MAJORITY
BURNING DOWN THE FOREMAN OF CONTROL

SILENCE IS THE ENEMY
AGAINST YOUR URGENCY
SO RALLY UP THE DEMONS OF YOUR SOUL

THE INSURGENCY WILL RISE
WHEN THE BLOODS BEEN SACRIFICED
DON'T BE BLINDED BY THE LIES
IN YOUR EYES.

VIOLENCE IS AN ENERGY
FROM HERE TO ETERNITY
VIOLENCE IS AN ENERGY
SILENCE IS THE ENEMY
SO GIMME GIMME REVOLUTION

¡VIVA LA GLORIA!

HEY GLORIA
ARE YOU STANDING CLOSE TO THE EDGE?
LOOKOUT TO THE SETTING SUN
THE BRINK OF YOUR VISION
ETERNAL YOUTH IS
A LANDSCAPE OF THE LIE

THE CRACKS OF MY SKIN CAN PROVE
AS THE YEARS WILL TESTIFY
SAY YOUR PRAYERS AND LIGHT A FIRE
WERE GOING TO START A WAR
YOUR SLOGANS A GUN FOR HIRE
IT'S WHAT WE WAITED FOR

HEY GLORIA,

THIS IS WHY WERE ON THE EDGE
THE FIGHT OF OUR LIVES BEEN DRAWN TO
THIS UNDYING LOVE.

GLORIA, VIVA LA GLORIA
YOU BLAST YOUR NAME
IN GRAFFITI ON THE WALLS
FALLING THROUGH BROKEN GLASS THAT'S
SLASHING THROUGH YOUR SPIRIT
I CAN HEAR IT LIKE A JILTED CROWD.

GLORIA, WHERE ARE YOU GLORIA?
YOU FOUND A HOME
IN ALL YOUR SCARS AND AMMUNITION
YOU MADE YOUR BED IN SALAD DAYS
AMONGST THE RUIN
ASHES TO ASHES OF OUR YOUTH

SHE SMASHED HER KNUCKLES INTO WINTER
AS AUTUMNS WIND FADES INTO BLACK
SHE IS THE SAINT ON ALL THE SINNERS
THE ONE THAT'S FALLEN THROUGH THE CRACKS
SO DON'T PUT AWAY YOUR BURNING LIGHT

GLORIA, WHERE ARE YOU GLORIA?
DON'T LOSE YOUR FAITH
TO YOUR LOST NAIVETE
WEATHER THE STORM AND DON'T LOOK
BACK ON LAST NOVEMBER
WHEN YOUR BANNERS WERE BURNING DOWN

GLORIA, VIVA LA GLORIA
SEND ME YOUR AMNESTY DOWN
TO THE BROKEN HEARTED
BRING US THE SEASON
THAT WE ALWAYS WILL REMEMBER
DON'T LET THE BONFIRES GO OUT

SO GLORIA,
SEND OUT YOUR MESSAGE OF THE LIGHT
THAT SHADOWS IN THE NIGHT.
GLORIA, WHERE'S YOUR UNDYING LOVE?
TELL ME THE STORY OF YOUR LIFE.

CHRISTIAN'S INFERNO

I GOT UNDER THE GRIP
BETWEEN THE MODERN HELL
I GOT THE REJECTION LETTER IN THE MAIL
AND IT WAS ALREADY RIPPED TO SHREDS.

SEASONS IN A RUIN AND
THIS BITTER PILL IS CHASED WITH BLOOD
THERE'S FIRE IN MY VEINS
AND IT'S POURING OUT LIKE A FLOOD

CHRISTIAN'S INFERNO
CHRISTIAN'S INFERNO

THIS DIABOLIC STATE
IS GRACING MY EXISTENCE
LIKE A CATASTROPHIC BABY
MAYBE MAYBE YOU'RE THE CHEMICAL REACTION
I AM THE ATOM BOMB
I AM THE CHOSEN ONE
TOXIN YOUR RESERVOIR
AND THEN RETURN MAN TO APE

CHRISTIAN'S INFERNO
CHRISTIAN'S INFERNO

BEFORE THE LOBOTOMY

DREAMING
I AM ONLY DREAMING
OF ANOTHER PLACE AND TIME
WHERE MY FAMILY'S FROM.
SINGING
I CAN HEAR THEM SINGING,
WHEN THE RAIN HAD WASHED AWAY
ALL THESE SCATTERED DREAMS
DYING
EVERYONES REMINDED
HEARTS ARE WASHED IN MISERY
DRENCHED IN GASOLINE
LAUGHTER
THERE IS NO MORE LAUGHTER
SONGS OF YESTERDAY
NOW LIVE IN THE UNDERGROUND
LIFE BEFORE THE LOBOTOMY
CHRISTIAN SANG THE EULOGY
SIGN MY LOVE A LOST MEMORY
FROM THE END OF THE CENTURY

WELL IT'S ENOUGH TO MAKE YOU SICK
TO CAST A STONE AND THROW A BRICK
WHEN THE SKY IS FALLING DOWN
IT BURNED YOUR DREAMS INTO THE GROUND
CHRISTIAN'S LESSON
IS WHAT HE'S BEEN SOLD
WE ARE NORMAL AND SELF-CONTROLLED
REMEMBER TO LEARN TO FORGET
WHISKEY SHOTS AND CHEAP CIGARETTES

WELL I'M NOT STONED
I'M JUST FUCKED UP
I GOT SO HIGH I CANT STAND UP
I'M NOT CURSED CAUSE
I'VE BEEN BLESSED
I'M NOT IN LOVE CAUSE I'M A MESS

LIKE REFUGEES
WE'RE LOST LIKE REFUGEES
LIKE REFUGEES
WE'RE LOST LIKE REFUGEES
THE BRUTALITY OF REALITY
IS THE FREEDOM THAT KEEPS ME FROM
DREAMING
I WAS ONLY DREAMING
OF ANOTHER PLACE AND TIME
WHERE MY FAMILY'S FROM.
SINGING
I CAN HEAR THEM SINGING
WHEN THE RAIN HAD WASHED AWAY
ALL THESE SCATTERED DREAMS
DYING
EVERYONES REMINDED
HEARTS ARE WASHED IN MISERY
DRENCHED IN GASOLINE
LAUGHTER
THERE IS NO MORE LAUGHTER
SONGS OF YESTERDAY
NOW LIVE IN THE UNDERGROUND

I TEXT A POSTCARD, SENT TO YOU
DID IT GO THROUGH?
SENDING ALL MY LOVE TO YOU.
YOU ARE THE MOONLIGHT OF MY LIFE EVERY NIGHT
GIVING ALL MY LOVE TO YOU
MY BEATING HEART BELONGS TO YOU
I WALKED FOR MILES 'TIL I FOUND YOU
I'M HERE TO HONOR YOU
IF I LOSE EVERYTHING IN THE FIRE
I'M SENDING ALL MY LOVE TO YOU.

WITH EVERY BREATH THAT I AM WORTH
HERE ON EARTH
I'M SENDING ALL MY LOVE TO YOU.
SO IF YOU DARE TO SECOND GUESS
YOU CAN REST ASSURED
THAT ALL MY LOVE'S FOR YOU
MY BEATING HEART BELONGS TO YOU
I WALKED FOR MILES 'TIL I FOUND YOU
I'M HERE TO HONOR YOU
IF I LOSE EVERYTHING IN THE FIRE
I'M SENDING ALL MY LOVE TO YOU.

MY BEATING HEART BELONGS TO YOU
I WALKED FOR MILES 'TIL I FOUND YOU
I'M HERE TO HONOR YOU
IF I LOSE EVERYTHING IN THE FIRE
DID I EVER MAKE IT THROUGH?

EAST JESUS NOWHERE

RAISE YOUR HANDS NOW TO TESTIFY
YOUR CONFESSION WILL BE CRUCIFIED
YOU'RE A SACRIFICIAL SUICIDE
LIKE A DOG THAT'S BEEN SODOMIZED
STAND UP! - ALL THE WHITE BOYS
SIT DOWN! - AND THE BLACK GIRLS
YOU'RE THE SOLDIERS OF THE NEW WORLD

PUT YOUR FAITH IN A MIRACLE
AND IT'S NON-DENOMINATIONAL
JOIN THE CHOIR WE WILL BE SINGING
IN THE CHURCH OF WISHFUL THINKING

A FIRE BURNS TODAY
OF BLASPHEMY AND GENOCIDE
THE SIRENS OF DECAY
WILL INFILTRATE THE FAITH FANATICS

OH BLESS ME LORD FOR I HAVE SINNED
IT'S BEEN A LIFETIME SINCE I LAST CONFESSED
I THREW MY CRUTCHES IN "THE RIVER
OF A SHADOW OF DOUBT"
AND I'LL BE DRESSED IN MY SUNDAY BEST

SAY A PRAYER FOR THE FAMILY
DROP A COIN FOR HUMANITY
AIN'T THIS UNIFORM SO FLATTERING?
I NEVER ASKED YOU A GOD DAMNED THING

DON'T TEST ME
SECOND GUESS ME
PROTEST ME
YOU WILL DISAPPEAR

I WANT TO KNOW WHO'S ALLOWED TO BREED
ALL THE DOGS WHO NEVER LEARNED TO READ
MISSIONARY POLITICIANS
AND THE COPS OF A NEW RELIGION

A FIRE BURNS TODAY
OF BLASPHEMY AND GENOCIDE
THE SIRENS OF DECAY
WILL INFILTRATE THE INSIDE

PEACEMAKER

WELL, IVE GOT A FEVER
A NON-BELIEVER
I'M IN A STATE OF GRACE
FOR I AM THE CEASAR
I'M GONNA SEIZE THE DAY
WELL, CALL OF THE BANSHEE HEY HEY
HEY HEY HEY HEY HEY
AS GOD AS MY WITNESS
THE INFIDELS ARE GONNA PAY

WELL, CALL THE ASSASSIN
THE ORGASM
A SPASM OF LOVE AND HATE
FOR WHAT WILL DIVIDE US?
THE RIGHTEOUS AND THE MEEK
WELL, CALL OF THE WILD HEY HEY
HEY HEY HEY HEY HEY
DEATH TO THE GIRL
AT THE END OF THE SERENADE

VENDETTA, SWEET VENDETTA
THIS BERETTA OF THE NIGHT
THIS FIRE AND THE DESIRE
SHOTS RINGING OUT ON A HOLY PARASITE

I AM A KILLJOY FROM DETROIT
I DRINK FROM A WELL OF RAGE
I FEED OFF THE WEAKNESS
WITH ALL MY LOVE

CALL UP THE CAPTAIN HEY HEY
HEY HEY HEY HEY HEY
DEATH TO THE LOVER THAT YOU WERE
DREAMING OF

THIS IS A STAND OFF
A MOLOTOV COCKTAIL
ON THE HOUSE
YOU THOUGHT I WAS A WRITE OFF
YOU BETTER THINK AGAIN
CALL THE PEACEMAKER HEY HEY
HEY HEY HEY HEY HEY
I'M GONNA SEND YOU BACK TO THE PLACE
WHERE IT ALL BEGAN

WELL NOW THE CARETAKER'S
THE UNDERTAKER
NOW I'M GONNA GO OUT
AND GET THE PEACEMAKER
THIS IS THE NEO
ST. VALENTINES MASSACRE
WELL CALL UP THE GAZA HEY HEY
HEY HEY HEY HEY HEY
DEATH TO THE ONES
AT THE END OF THE SERENADE
WELL, DEATH TO THE ONES
AT THE END OF THE SERENADE

LAST OF THE AMERICAN GIRLS

SHE PUTS HER MAKEUP ON
LIKE GRAFFITI ON THE WALLS OF THE HEARTLAND
SHE'S GOT HER LITTLE BOOK OF CONSPIRACIES
RIGHT IN HER HAND
SHE IS PARANOID LIKE
ENDANGERED SPECIES HEADED INTO
EXTINCTION
SHE IS ONE OF A KIND
SHE'S THE LAST OF THE AMERICAN GIRLS

SHE WEARS HER OVERCOAT
FOR THE COMING OF THE NUCLEAR WINTER
SHE IS RIDING HER BIKE
LIKE A FUGITIVE OF CRITICAL MASS
SHE'S ON A HUNGER STRIKE
FOR THE ONES WHO WON'T MAKE IT FOR DINNER

SHE MAKES ENOUGH TO SURVIVE
FOR A HOLIDAY OF WORKING CLASS

SHE'S A RUNAWAY OF THE ESTABLISHMENT
INCORPORATED
SHE WON'T COOPERATE
SHE'S THE LAST OF THE AMERICAN GIRLS

SHE PLAYS HER VINYL RECORDS
SINGING SONGS ON THE EVE OF DESTRUCTION
SHE'S A SUCKER FOR
ALL THE CRIMINALS BREAKING THE LAWS
SHE WILL COME IN FIRST
FOR THE END OF WESTERN CIVILIZATION

SHE'S AN ENDLESS WAR
LIKE A HERO FOR THE LOST CAUSE
LIKE A HURRICANE
IN THE HEART OF THE DEVASTATION
SHE'S A NATURAL DISASTER
SHE'S THE LAST OF THE AMERICAN GIRLS

SHE PUTS HER MAKEUP ON
LIKE GRAFFITI
ON THE WALLS OF THE HEARTLAND
SHE'S GOT HER LITTLE BOOK OF CONSPIRACIES
RIGHT IN HER HAND
SHE WILL COME IN FIRST
FOR THE END OF WESTERN CIVILIZATION
SHE'S A NATURAL DISASTER
SHE'S THE LAST OF THE AMERICAN GIRLS

MURDER CITY

DESPERATE
BUT NOT HOPELESS
I FEEL SO USELESS
IN THE MURDER CITY

DESPERATE
BUT NOT HELPLESS
THE CLOCK STRIKES MIDNIGHT
IN THE MURDER CITY

I'M WIDE AWAKE
AFTER THE RIOT
THIS DEMONSTRATION
OF OUR ANGUISH
~~THIS EMPTY LAUGHTER~~
HAS NO REASON
LIKE A BOTTLE
OF YOUR FAVORITE POISON

WE ARE THE LAST CALL
AND WE'RE SO PATHETIC
~~CHRISTIAN'S CRYING~~
IN THE BATHROOM
AND I JUST WANT TO
BUM A CIGARETTE
WE'VE COME SO FAR,
WE'VE BEEN SO WASTED
IT'S WRITTEN
ALL OVER OUR FACES

¿VIVA LA GLORIA? [LITTLE GIRL]

LITTLE GIRL, LITTLE GIRL
WHY ARE YOU CRYING?
INSIDE YOUR RESTLESS SOUL
YOUR HEART IS DYING.
LITTLE ONE, LITTLE ONE
YOUR SOUL IS PURGING
OF LOVE AND RAZOR BLADES
YOUR BLOOD IS SURGING

RUNAWAY
FROM THE RIVER TO THE STREET
AND FIND YOURSELF
WITH YOUR FACE IN THE GUTTER
YOUR A STRAY FOR THE SALVATION ARMY
THERE IS NO PLACE LIKE HOME
WHEN YOU GOT NO PLACE TO GO

LITTLE GIRL, LITTLE GIRL
YOUR LIFE IS CALLING
THE CHARLATANS AND SAINTS
OF YOUR ABANDON

LITTLE ONE LITTLE ONE
THE SKY IS FALLING
THE LIFEBOAT OF DECEPTION
IS NOW SAILING
IN THE WAKE ALL THE WAY
NO RHYME OR REASON

YOUR BLOODSHOT EYES
WILL SHOW YOUR HEART OF TREASON
LITTLE GIRL LITTLE GIRL
YOU DIRTY LIAR
YOU'RE JUST A JUNKIE
PREACHING TO THE CHOIR

RUNAWAY
FROM THE RIVER TO THE STREET
AND FIND YOURSELF
WITH YOUR FACE IN THE GUTTER
YOUR A STRAY FOR THE SALVATION ARMY
THERE IS NO PLACE LIKE HOME
WHEN YOU GOT NO PLACE TO GO

THE TRACES OF BLOOD
ALWAYS FOLLOW YOU HOME
LIKE THE MASCARA TEARS
FROM YOUR GETAWAY
YOUR WALKING WITH BLISTERS
AND RUNNING WITH SHEARS

SO UNHOLY.

SISTER OF GRACE.

RESTLESS HEART SYNDROME

I'VE GOT A REALLY BAD DISEASE
IT'S GOT ME BEGGING ON MY HANDS AND KNEES
TAKE ME TO THE EMERGENCY
CAUSE SOMETHING SEEMS TO BE MISSING
SOMEBODY TAKE THE PAIN AWAY
IT'S LIKE AN ULCER BLEEDING IN MY BRAIN
SEND ME TO THE PHARMACY
SO I CAN LOSE MY MEMORY

I'M ELATED
MEDICATED
LORD KNOWS I TRIED TO FIND A WAY TO RUN AWAY.

I THINK THEY FOUND ANOTHER CURE
FOR BROKEN HEARTS AND FEELING INSECURE
YOU'D BE SURPRISED WHAT I ENDURE
WHAT MAKES YOU FEEL SO SELF-ASSURED

I NEED TO FIND A PLACE TO HIDE
YOU NEVER KNOW WHAT COULD BE WAITING OUTSIDE
THE ACCIDENTS THAT YOU COULD FIND
IT'S LIKE SOME KIND OF SUICIDE

SO WHAT AILS YOU IS WHAT IMPALES YOU
I FEEL LIKE I'VE BEEN CRUCIFIED TO BE SATISFIED

I'M ELATED
MEDICATED
I AM MY OWN WORST ENEMY
SO WHAT AILS YOU IS WHAT IMPALES YOU
YOU ARE YOUR OWN WORST ENEMY
YOU'RE A VICTEM OF THE SYSTEM

I'M A VICTIM OF MY SYMPTOM
I AM MY OWN WORST ENEMY
YOU'RE A VICTIM OF YOUR SYMPTOM
YOU ARE YOUR OWN WORST ENEMY
KNOW YOUR ENEMY.

HORSESHOES AND HANDGRENADES

I'M NOT FUCKING AROUND
I THINK I'M COMING OUT
ALL THE DECEIVERS AND CHEATERS
I THINK WE'VE GOT A BLEEDER RIGHT NOW
WANT YOU TO SLAP ME AROUND
WANT YOU TO KNOCK ME OUT
WELL, YOU MISSED ME KISSED ME
NOW YOU BETTER KICK ME DOWN

MAYBE YOU'RE THE RUNNER UP
BUT THE FIRST ONE TO LOSE THE RACE
ALMOST ONLY REALLY COUNTS IN
HORSESHOES AND HAND GRENADES
I'M GONNA BURN IT ALL DOWN
I'M GONNA RIP IT OUT
WELL, EVERYTHING THAT YOU EMPLOY
WAS MEANT FOR ME TO DESTROY
TO THE GROUND NOW
SO DON'T YOU FUCK ME AROUND
BECAUSE I'LL SHOOT YOU DOWN
I'M GONNA DRINK, FIGHT AND FUCK
AND PUSHING MY LUCK
ALL THE TIME NOW

DEMOLITION, SELF-DESTRUCTION
WHAT TO ANNIHILATE
THE AGE-OLD CONTRADICTION
DEMOLITION, SELF-DESTRUCTION
WHAT TO ANNIHILATE
THE OLD AGE

I'M NOT FUCKING AROUND
I THINK I'M COMING OUT
I'M A HATER, A TRAITOR
IN A PAIR OF CHUCK TAYLORS RIGHT NOW
I'M NOT FUCKING AROUND
G-L-O-R-I-A

THE STATIC AGE

CAN YOU HEAR THE SOUND
OF THE STATIC NOISE
BLASTING OUT IN STEREO
CATER TO THE CLASS AND THE PARANOID

MUSIC TO MY NERVOUS SYSTEM
ADVERTISING LOVE AND RELIGION
MURDER ON THE AIRWAVES
SLOGANS ON THE BRINK OF CORRUPTION

VISION OF BLASPHEMY, WAR AND PEACE
SCREAMING AT YOU

I CAN'T SEE A THING IN THE VIDEO
I CAN'T HEAR A SOUND ON THE RADIO
IN STEREO IN THE STATIC AGE

BILLBOARD ON THE RISE
IN THE DAWN'S LANDSCAPE
WORKING YOUR INSANITY
TRAGIC A'LA MADNESS AND CONCRETE
COCA COLA EXECUTION
CONSCIOUS ON A CROSS AND
YOUR HEARTS IN A VICE
SQUEEZING OUT YOUR STATE OF MIND
ARE WHAT YOU OWN THAT YOU CANNOT BUY
WHAT A FUCKING TRAGEDY, STRATEGY
SCREAMING AT YOU.

HEY HEY IT'S THE STATIC AGE
THIS IS HOW THE WEST WAS WON
HEY HEY IT'S THE STATIC AGE
MILLENIUM

ALL I WANT TO KNOW
IS A GOD DAMNED THING
NOT WHAT'S IN THE MEDICINE
ALL I WANT TO DO IS
I WANT TO BREATHE
BATTERIES ARE NOT INCLUDED
WHAT'S THE LATEST WAY
THAT A MAN CAN DIE
SCREAMING HALLELUJAH?

SINGING OUT
"THE DAWN'S EARLY LIGHT"

THE SILENCE OF THE ROTTEN,
FORGOTTEN
SCREAMING AT YOU.

I CAN'T SEE A THING IN THE VIDEO
I CAN'T HEAR A SOUND ON THE RADIO
IN STEREO IN THE STATIC AGE

21 GUNS

DO YOU KNOW WHAT'S WORTH FIGHTING FOR
WHEN IT'S NOT WORTH DYING FOR?
DOES IT TAKE YOUR BREATH AWAY
AND YOU FEEL YOURSELF SUFFOCATING
DOES THE PAIN WEIGH OUT THE PRIDE?
AND YOU LOOK FOR A PLACE TO HIDE
DID SOMEONE BREAK YOUR HEART INSIDE
YOU'RE IN RUINS

ONE, 21 GUNS
LAY DOWN YOUR ARMS
GIVE UP THE FIGHT
ONE, 21 GUNS
THROW UP YOUR ARMS INTO THE SKY,
YOU AND I

WHEN YOU'RE AT THE END OF THE ROAD
AND YOU LOST ALL SENSE OF CONTROL
AND YOUR THOUGHTS HAVE TAKEN THEIR TOLL
WHEN YOUR MIND BREAKS THE SPIRIT OF YOUR SOUL
YOUR FAITH WALKS ON BROKEN GLASS
AND THE HANGOVER DOESN'T PASS
NOTHING'S EVER BUILT TO LAST
YOU'RE IN RUINS.

DID YOU TRY TO LIVE ON YOUR OWN
WHEN YOU BURNED DOWN THE HOUSE AND HOME
DID YOU STAND TOO CLOSE TO THE FIRE?
LIKE A LIAR LOOKING FOR FORGIVENESS FROM A STONE

WHEN IT'S TIME TO LIVE AND LET DIE
AND YOU CAN'T GET ANOTHER TRY
SOMETHING INSIDE THIS HEART HAS DIED
YOU'RE IN RUINS.

AMERICAN EULOGY XIII

SING US A SONG OF THE CENTURY
IT SINGS LIKE AMERICAN EULOGY
THE DAWN OF MY LOVE AND CONSPIRACY
[illegible]GOTTEN HOPE AND THE CLASS OF 13
TELL ME [illegible]TON INTO THAT GOOD NIGHT
[illegible] A SONG FOR ME

A. MASS HYSTERIA

MASS HYSTERIA
RED ALERT IS THE COLOR OF PANIC
ELEVATED TO THE POINT OF STATIC
BEATING INTO THE HEARTS OF THE FANATICS
AND THE NEIGHBORHOOD'S A LOADED GUN
IDLE THOUGHT LEAD TO
FULL-THROTTLE SCREAMING
AND THE WELFARE IS ASPHYXIATING
MASS CONFUSION IS ALL THE NEW RAGE
AND IT'S CREATING A FEEDING GROUND
FOR THE BOTTOM FEEDERS OF HYSTERIA
TRUE SOUNDS OF MANIACAL LAUGHTER
AND THE DEAF MUTE IS
MISLEADING THE CHOIR
THE PUNCHLINE IS A NATURAL DISASTER
AND IT'S SUNG BY THE UNEMPLOYED
FIGHT FIRE WITH A RIOT
THE CLASS WAR IS HANGING ON A WIRE
BECAUSE THE MARTYR
IS A COMPULSIVE LIAR
WHEN HE SAID
"IT'S JUST A BUNCH OF NIGGERS
THROWING GAS INTO THE HYSTERIA"

THERE'S A DISTURBANCE ON THE OCEANSIDE
THEY TAPPED INTO THE RESERVE
THE STATIC RESPONSE IS SO UNCLEAR NOW
MAYDAY THIS IS NOT A TEST!
AS THE NEIGHBORHOOD BURNS,
AMERICA IS FALLING
VIGILANTES WARNING YA,
CALLING CHRISTIAN AND GLORIA

B. MODERN WORLD

I'M A FUGITIVE SON
IN THE ERA OF DISSENT
A HOSTAGE OF THE SOUL
ON A STRIKE TO PAY THE RENT
THE LAST OF THE REBELS
WITHOUT A COMMON GROUND
I'M GONNA LIGHT A FIRE
INTO THE UNDERGROUND

I DON'T WANT TO LIVE
IN THE MODERN WORLD

I AM A NATION
WITHOUT BUREAUCRATIC TIES
DENY THE ALLEGATION AS IT'S WRITTEN

I WANT TO TAKE A RIDE
TO THE GREAT DIVIDE
BEYOND THE "UP TO DATE"
AND THE NEO-GENTRIFIED
THE HIGH DEFINITION
FOR THE LOW RESIDENT
WHERE THE VALUE OF YOUR MIND
IS NOT HELD IN CONTEMPT
I CAN HEAR THE SOUND OF
A BEATING HEART
THAT BLEEDS BEHIND A SYSTEM
THAT'S FALLING APART
WITH MONEY TO BURN
ON A MINIMUM WAGE
I DON'T GIVE A SHIT
ABOUT THE MODERN AGE

I DON'T WANT TO LIVE
IN THE MODERN WORLD
MASS HYSTERIA

SEE THE LIGHT

I CROSSED THE RIVER
FELL INTO THE SEA
WHERE THE NON-BELIEVERS
GO BEYOND BELIEF
THEN I SCRATCHED THE SURFACE
IN THE MOUTH OF HELL
RUNNING OUT OF SERVICE
IN THE BLOOD I FELL

I JUST WANT TO SEE THE LIGHT
I DON'T WANT TO LOSE MY SIGHT
I JUST WANT TO SEE THE LIGHT
I NEED TO KNOW
WHAT'S WORTH THE FIGHT

I'VE BEEN WASTED
PILLS AND ALCOHOL
I'VE BEEN CHASING
DOWN THE POOL HALLS
I DRANK THE WATER
FROM A HURRICANE
I SET A FIRE
JUST TO SEE THE FLAME

I CROSSED THE DESERT
REACHING HIGHER GROUND
THEN I POUND THE PAVEMENT
TO TAKE THE LIARS DOWN
BUT IT'S GONE FOREVER
BUT NEVER TOO LATE
WHERE THE EVER AFTER
IS IN THE HANDS OF FATE

CONTENTS

ISBN-10: 0-7390-6205-0
ISBN-13: 978-0-7390-6205-0

SONG OF THE CENTURY

Lyrics by BILLIE JOE
Music by GREEN DAY

Moderately ♩ = 140

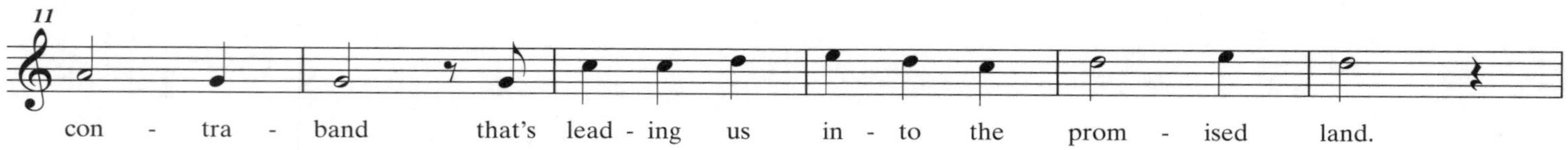

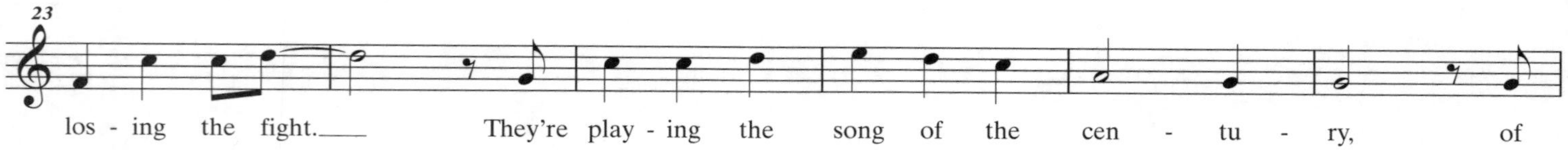

21st CENTURY BREAKDOWN

*Tune down 1/2 step:
⑥ = E♭ ③ = G♭
⑤ = A♭ ② = B♭
④ = D♭ ① = E♭

Lyrics by BILLIE JOE
Music by GREEN DAY

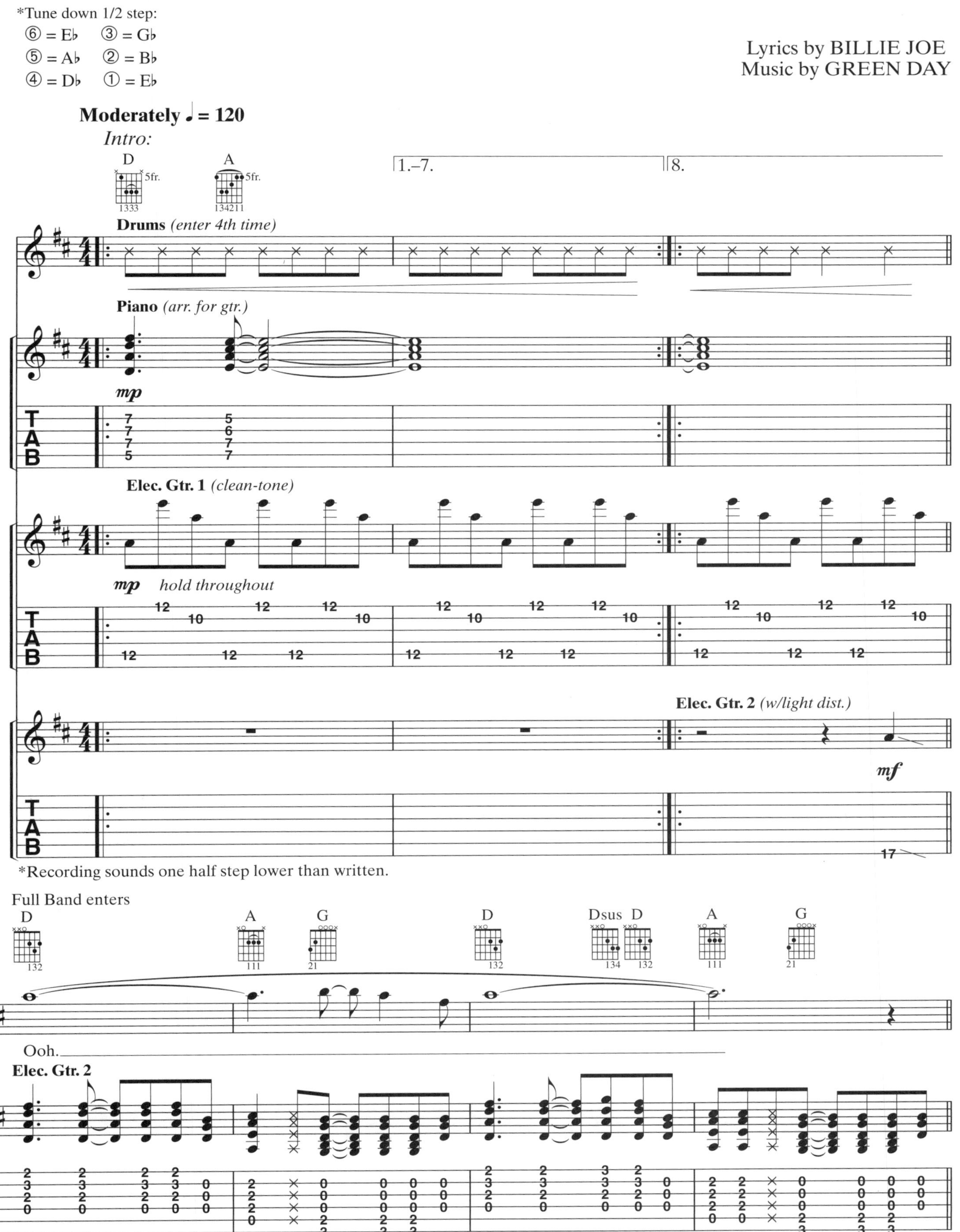

*Recording sounds one half step lower than written.

Verses 1 & 2:
D
A
G
D
Dsus D
Elec. Gtr. 2 cont. simile
1. Born in - to Nix - on, I was raised_ in hell,__ a wel - fare child where the
2. I was made of poi - son and blood,_ con - dem - na - tion is
A
G
D
A
G
team - sters dwelled._ The last one born__ and the first one to run,__
what I un - der - stood. Vid - e - o games_ to the tow - er's fall,__
D
Dsus
D
A
G
my town was blind from re - fin - er - y sun.____
home - land se - cu ri - ty could kill____ us all.____
Pre-chorus:
Bm
G
10fr.
Bm
G5
3fr.
A5
5fr.
My gen - er - a - tion is ze - ro, I nev - er made it as a work - ing class he - ro.
Elec. Gtr. 2
Chorus:
D
5fr.
A
5fr.
G
3fr.
D
5fr.
A
5fr.
G
3fr.
Twen - ty - first cen - tu - ry break - down, I once was lost but nev - er was_
Elec. Gtr. 2

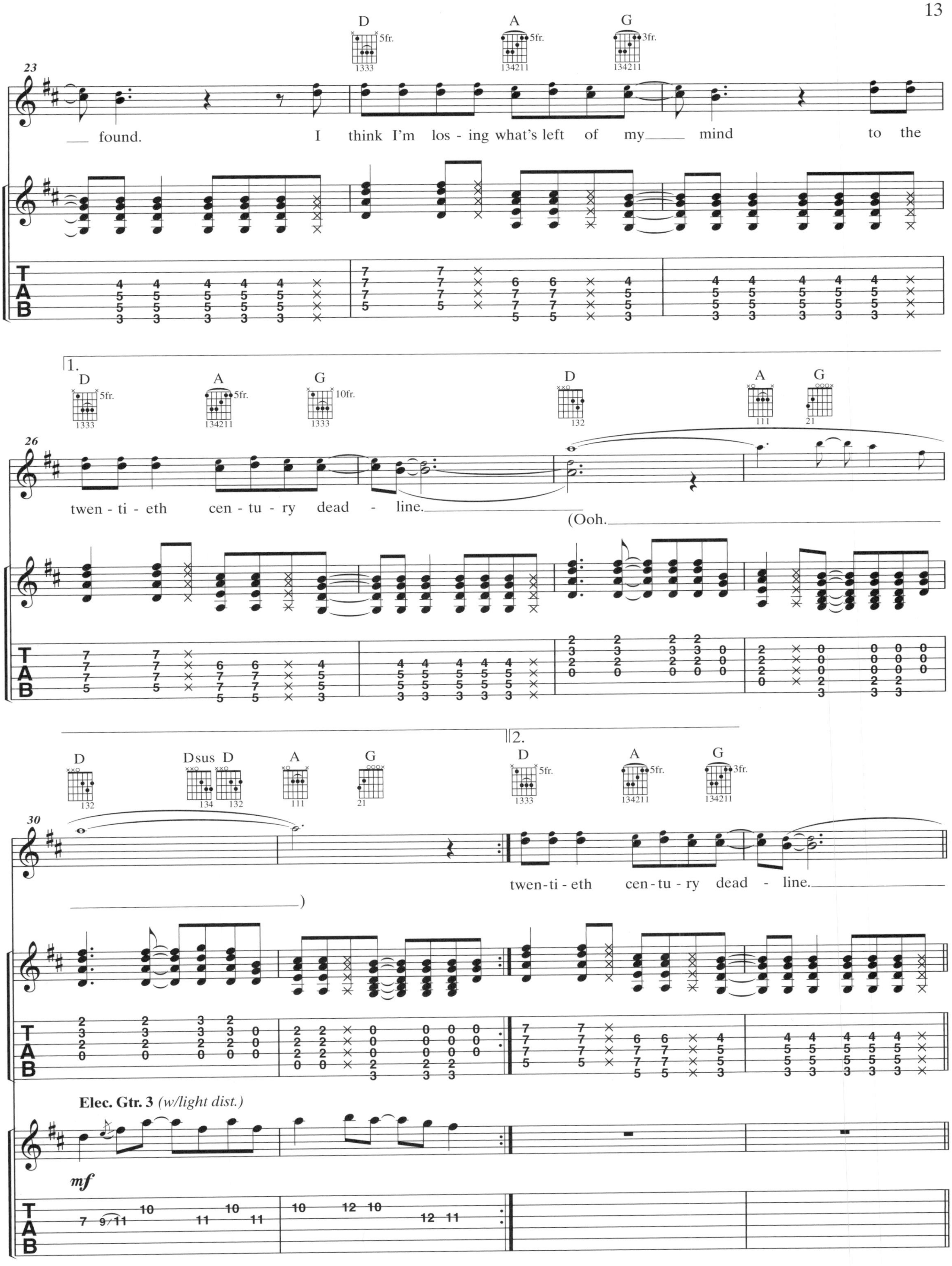
23
D 5fr. 1333
A 5fr. 134211
G 3fr. 134211
found. I think I'm los - ing what's left of my mind to the
1.
26
D 5fr. 1333
A 5fr. 134211
G 10fr. 1333
D 132
A 111
G 21
twen - ti - eth cen - tu - ry dead - line.
(Ooh.
30
D 132
Dsus 134
D 132
A 111
G 21
2.
D 5fr. 1333
A 5fr. 134211
G 3fr. 134211
)
twen - ti - eth cen - tu - ry dead - line.
Elec. Gtr. 3 (w/light dist.)
mf
TAB

Faster ♩ = 152

Instrumental:

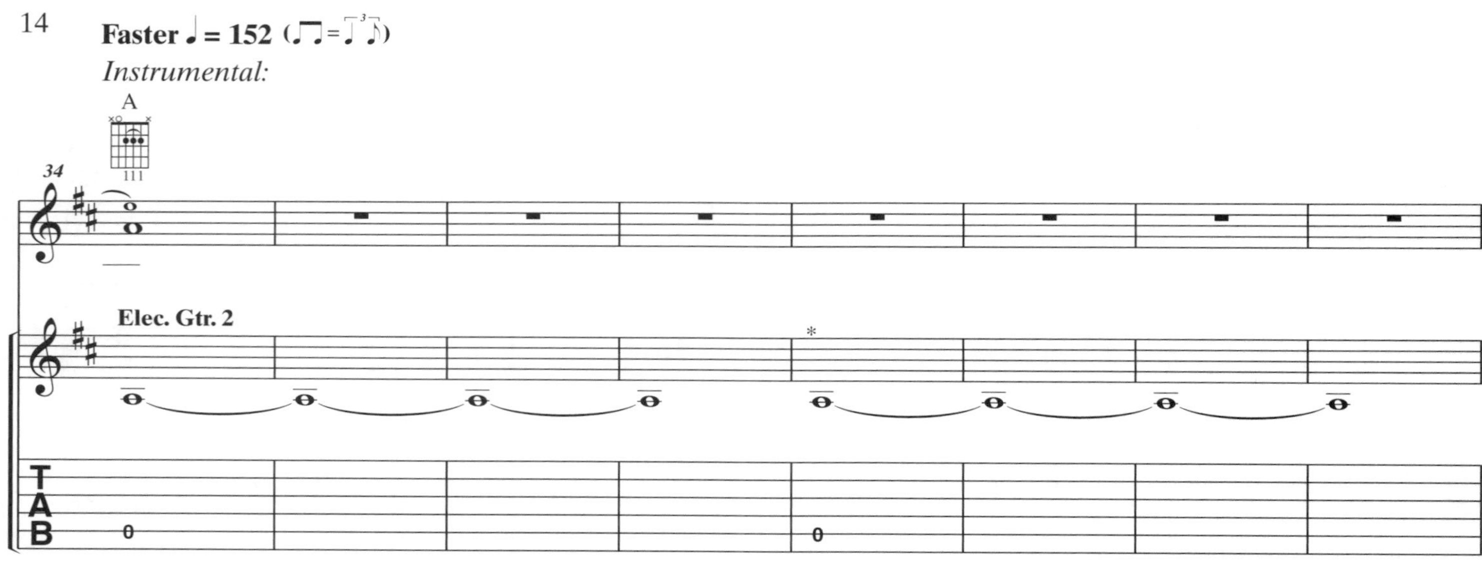

*Flick pickup selector switch back and forth while note rings out.

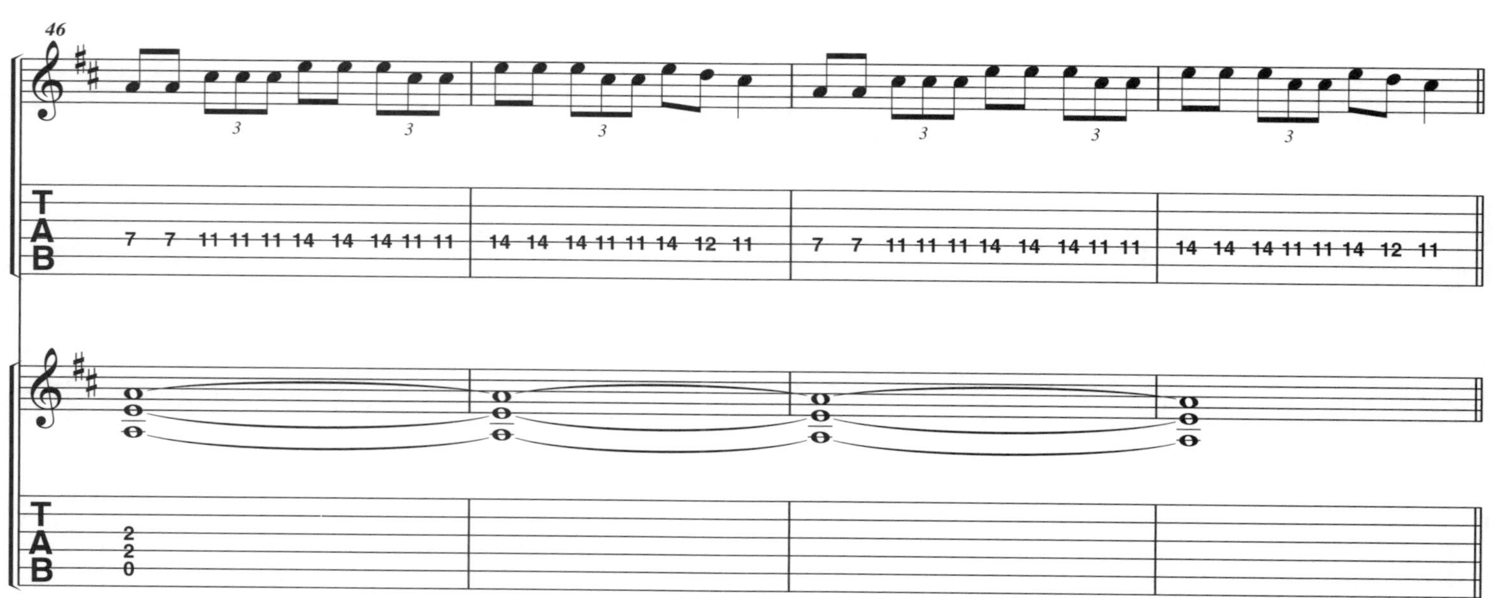

Verse 3:
A
D
A
D
We are the class of, the class of 'thir-teen, born in the year of hu-mil - i - ty.
Elec. Gtr. 2
We are the des-per-ate in the de-cline, raised by the bas-tards of nine - teen - six - ty -
Elec. Gtr. 3
nine.
5fr.

Verses 4 & 5:
D
G5
A5
D
4. My name is no one, the long lost son,
(5.) swal - lowed my pride and I choked on my faith. I've
Rhy. Fig. 1
Elec. Gtr. 2
A5
born on the Fourth of Ju - ly.
giv - en my heart and my soul. I've
end Rhy. Fig. 1
P.M.
w/Rhy. Fig. 1 (Elec. Gtr. 2) 3 times
D
G5
A5
D
Raised in the er - a of he - roes and cons, who left me for dead or a -
bro - ken my fin - gers and lied through my teeth, the pil - lar of dam - age con -

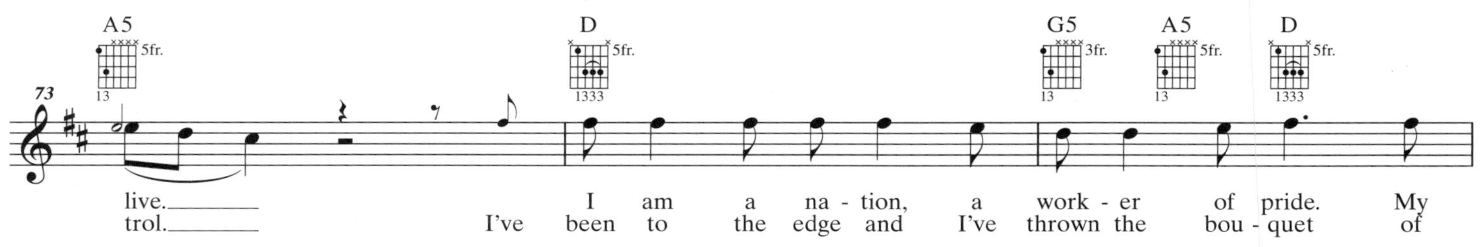
A5
D
G5
A5
D
live.
I am a na - tion, a work - er of pride. My
trol.
I've been to the edge and I've thrown the bou - quet of

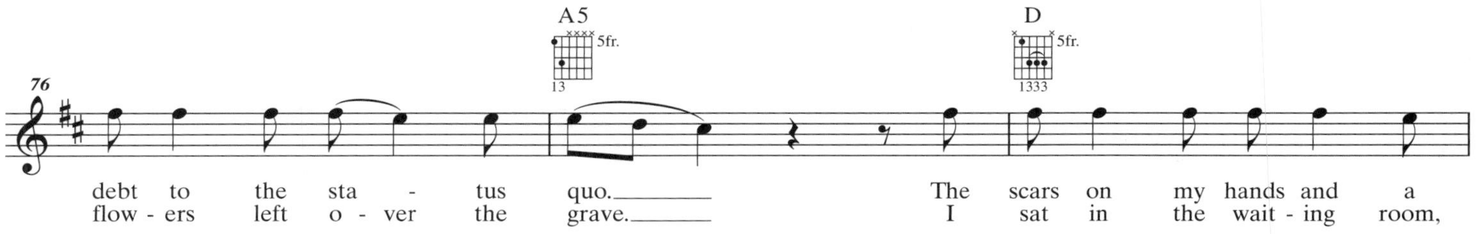
A5
D
debt to the sta - tus quo.
The scars on my hands and a
flow - ers left o - ver the grave.
I sat in the wait - ing room,

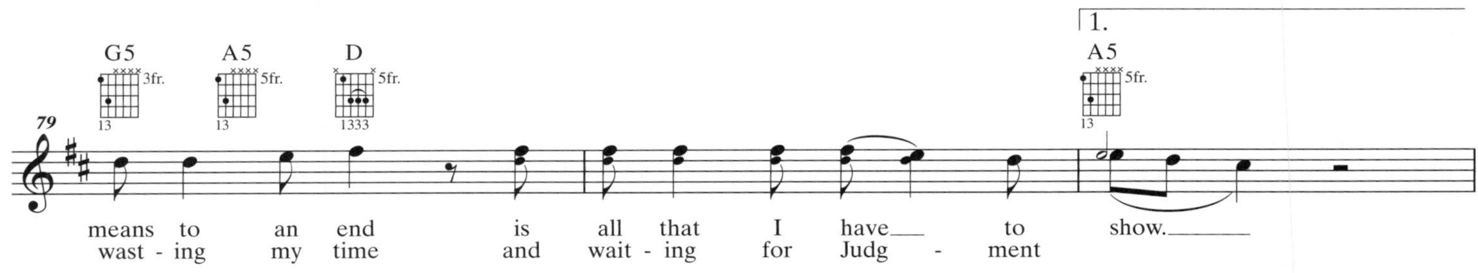
G5
A5
D
1.
A5
means to an end is all that I have to show.
wast - ing my time and wait - ing for Judg - ment

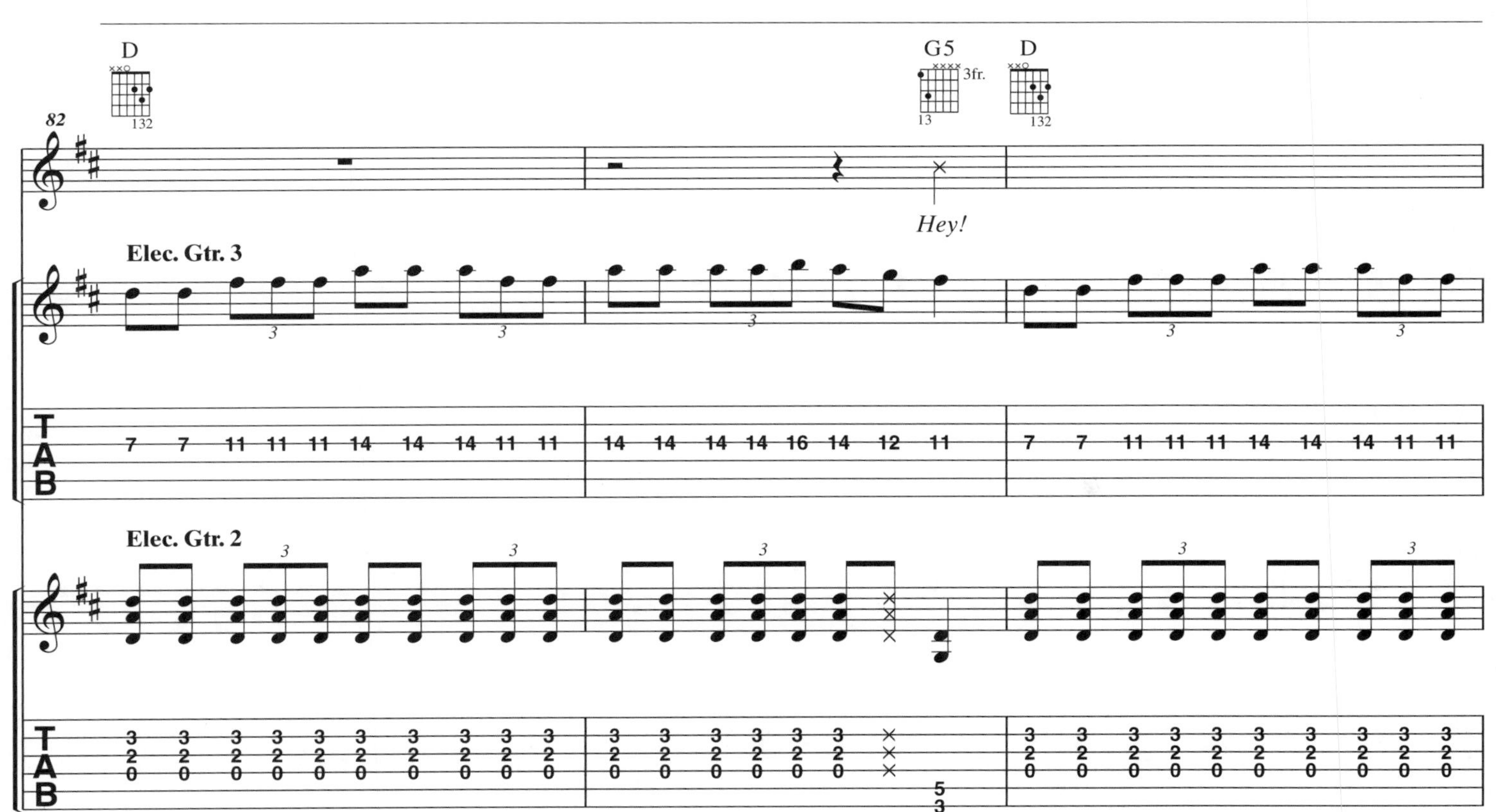
D
G5
D
Hey!
Elec. Gtr. 3
Elec. Gtr. 2

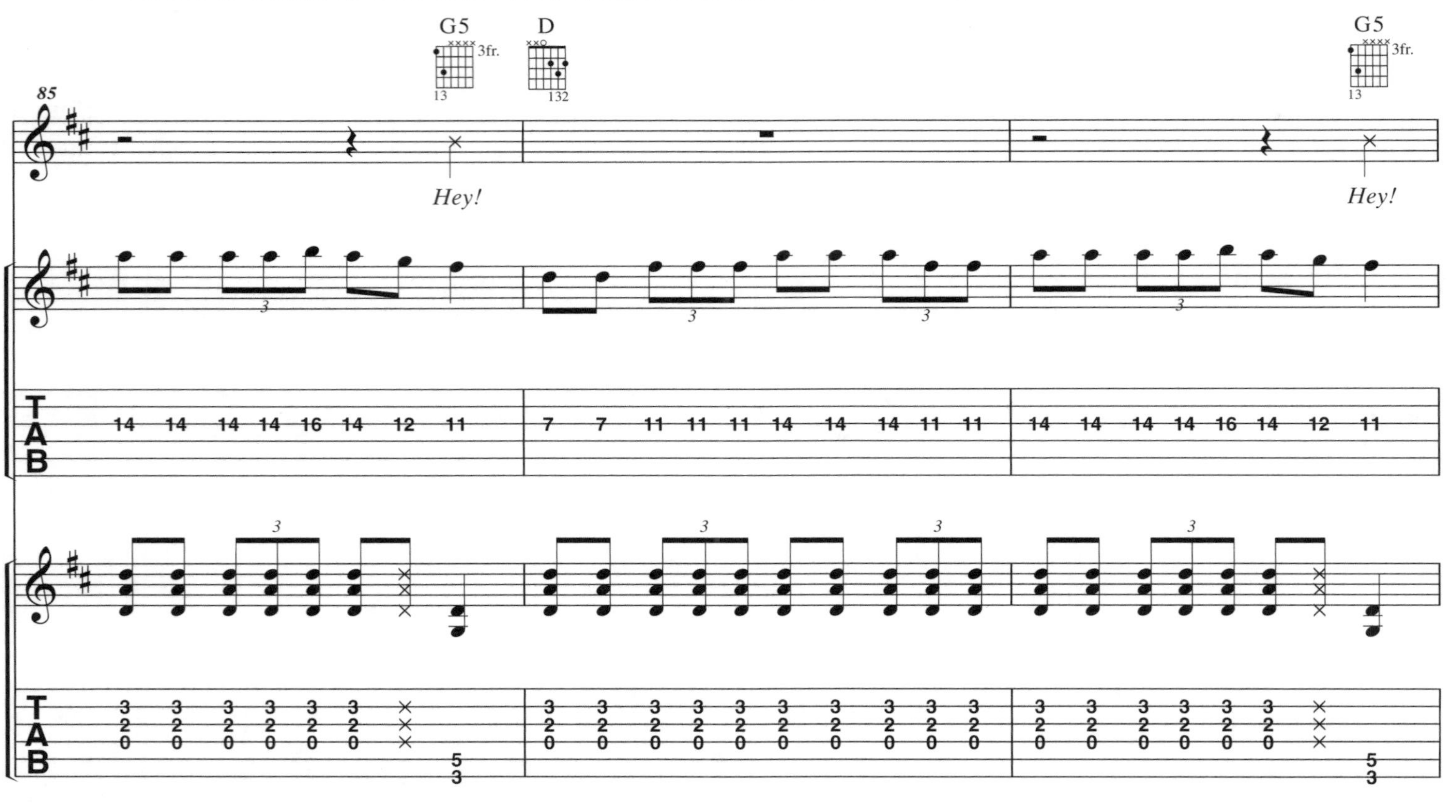

88

D

G5

2.

A5

5. I Day.

Bridge:

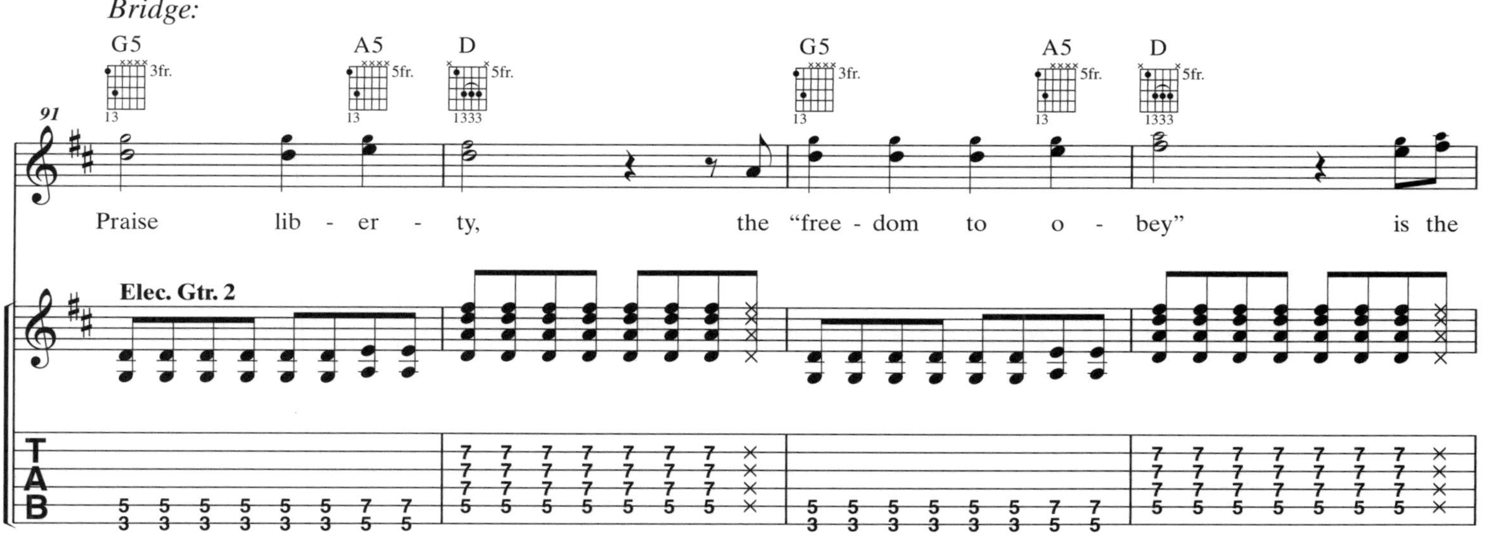
G5
3fr.
13
A5
5fr.
13
D
5fr.
1333
G5
3fr.
13
A5
5fr.
13
D
5fr.
1333
91
Praise lib - er - ty, the "free - dom to o - bey" is the
Elec. Gtr. 2
T
A
B
5 5 5 5 5 5 7 7
3 3 3 3 3 3 5 5
7 7 7 7 7 7 7
7 7 7 7 7 7 7
7 7 7 7 7 7 7
5 5 5 5 5 5 5
5 5 5 5 5 5 7 7
3 3 3 3 3 3 5 5
7 7 7 7 7 7 7
7 7 7 7 7 7 7
7 7 7 7 7 7 7
5 5 5 5 5 5 5

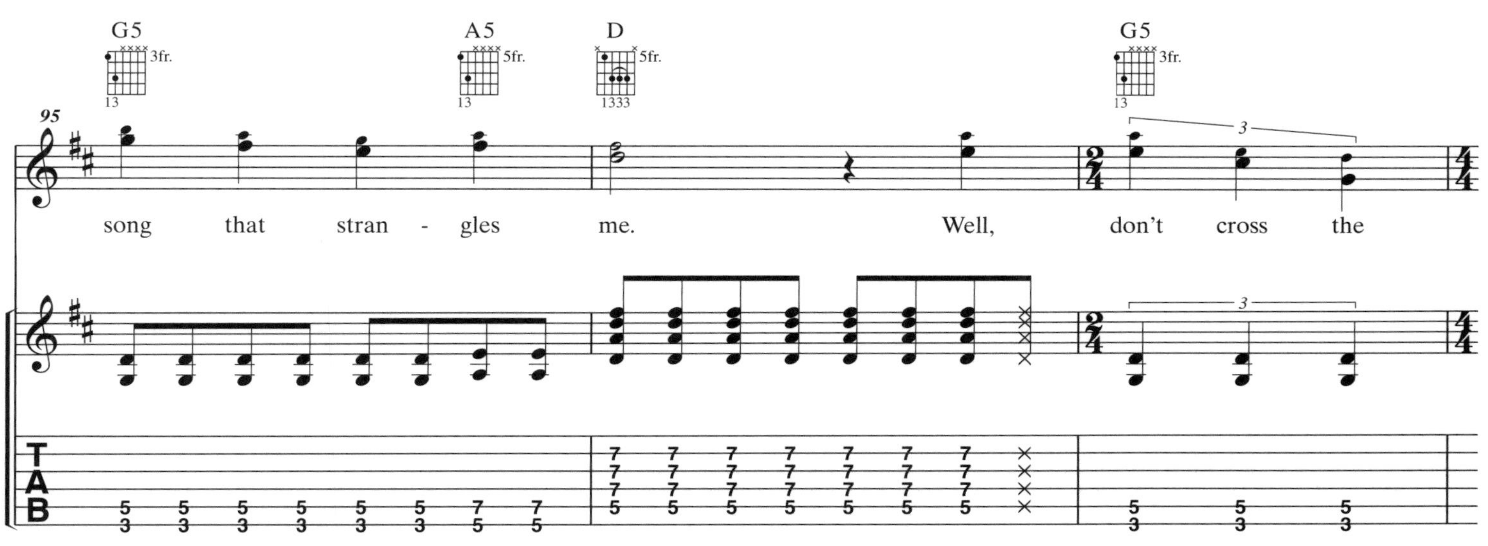
G5
3fr.
13
A5
5fr.
13
D
5fr.
1333
G5
3fr.
13
95
song that stran - gles me. Well, don't cross the
3
T
A
B
5 5 5 5 5 5 7 7
3 3 3 3 3 3 5 5
7 7 7 7 7 7 7
7 7 7 7 7 7 7
7 7 7 7 7 7 7
5 5 5 5 5 5 5
5 5 5
3 3 3

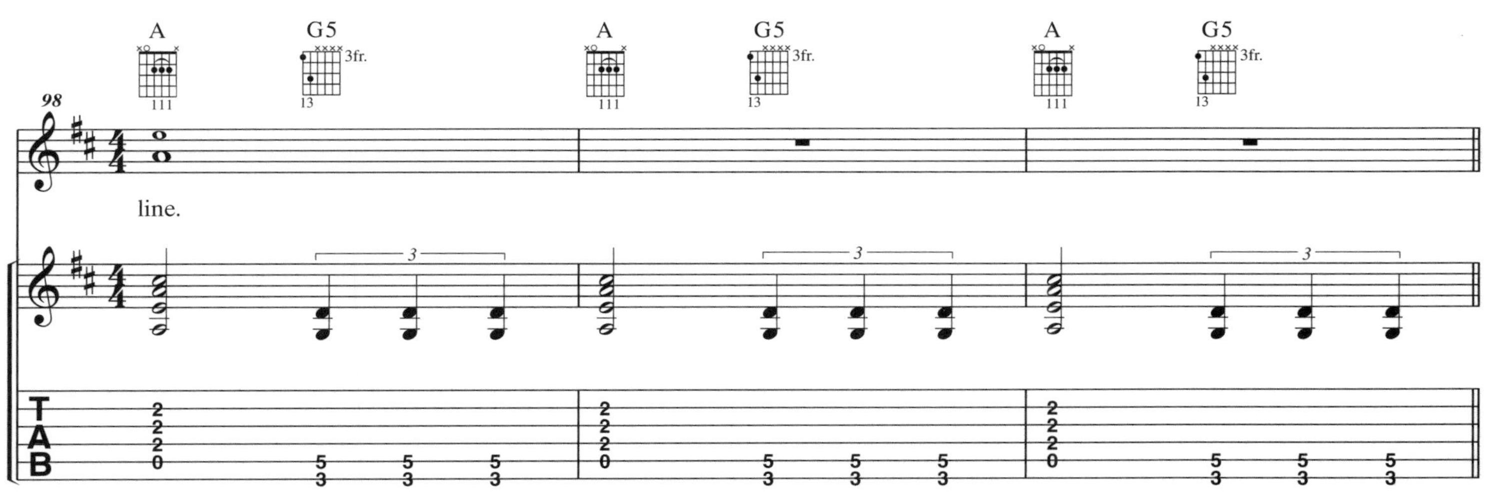
A
111
G5
3fr.
13
A
111
G5
3fr.
13
A
111
G5
3fr.
13
98
line.
3
3
3
T
A
B
2 2 2 0
5 5 5
3 3 3
2 2 2 0
5 5 5
3 3 3
2 2 2 0
5 5 5
3 3 3

Slower ♩ = 120
A
Elec. Gtr. 3
rit.
Elec. Gtr. 2
rit.
Interlude:
Slower ♩ = 72
D
A/C♯
Bm
A
G
B♭
D
Oh,
Elec. Gtr. 4 (w/light dist.)
mf
Elec. Gtr. 3
Elec. Gtr. 2

Outro:

D
A/C♯
Bm
A
G
B♭
D
dream, A-mer-i - ca,_ dream. I can't e - ven sleep from light's ear - ly__ dawn. Oh,_
Elec. Gtr. 3
Elec. Gtr. 2
N.C.
scream, A-mer - i - ca,_ scream. Be-lieve what_ you see from he-roes_ and_ cons.

KNOW YOUR ENEMY

Lyrics by BILLIE JOE
Music by GREEN DAY

Band enters
B
E5
B
F♯
7fr.
1342
133
got - ta know the en - e - my. (Rah eh!)
*
T
A
B
*Elec. Gtr. 1 dbld.
A5
5fr.
13
Do you know the en - e - my? Do you know your en - e - my? Well,
Rhy. Fig. 1
got - ta know the en - e - my. (Rah eh!)
end Rhy. Fig. 1
w/Rhy. Fig. 1 (Elec. Gtr. 1)
Do you know the en - e - my? Do you know your en - e - my? Well,
got - ta know the en - e - my. (Rah eh!)

Verse 1:
w/Rhy. Fig. 1 (Elec. Gtr. 1) 2 times
Vi-'lence is an en - er - gy, a - gainst the en - e - my, well, vi-'lence is an en - er - gy. (Rah
eh!) Bring - ing on the fu - ry, the cho - ir in - fan - try, re -
volt a - gainst the hon - or to o - bey. (Oh eh, oh eh.)
Verse 2:
w/Rhy. Fig. 1 (Elec. Gtr. 1) 2 times
O - ver-throw the ef - fi - gy, the vast ma - jor - i - ty, well, burn - ing down the fore - man of con -
trol. (Oh eh, oh eh.) Si - lence is the en - e - my, a - gainst your ur - gen - cy, so
ral - ly up the de - mons of your soul. (Oh eh, oh eh.)
Chorus:
w/Rhy. Fig. 1 (Elec. Gtr. 1) 2 times
Do you know the en - e - my? Do you know your en - e - my? Well,
got - ta know the en - e - my. (Rah eh!)

B E5 B E5 B A5
Do you know the en - e - my? Do you know your en - e - my? Well,
B E5 B F#
got - ta know the en - e - my. (Rah eh!) The in -
Bridge 1:
E5 B E5 B
sur - gen - cy will rise when the blood's been sac - ri - ficed.
Elec. Gtr. 2 (w/light dist.)
mf
Elec. Gtr. 1
E5 B
We'll be blind - ed by the lies in your eyes.

Elec. Gtr. 2 tacet 2 meas.
F♯
B
F♯
B
F♯
Say!
Guitar Solo:
w/Rhy. Fig. 1 (Elec. Gtr. 1) 2 times
B
E5
B
E5
B
A5
B
E5
B
Elec. Gtr. 2
F♯
B
E5
B
E5
B
A5
(Oh eh, oh eh.)
B
E5
B
F♯
(Oh eh, oh eh.)

E5
7fr.
133
B
7fr.
1342
61
T
A
B
Elec. Gtr. 1
Elec. Gtr. 2 tacet
F♯
1333
67
Well,
Rhy. Fig. 2
end Rhy. Fig. 2

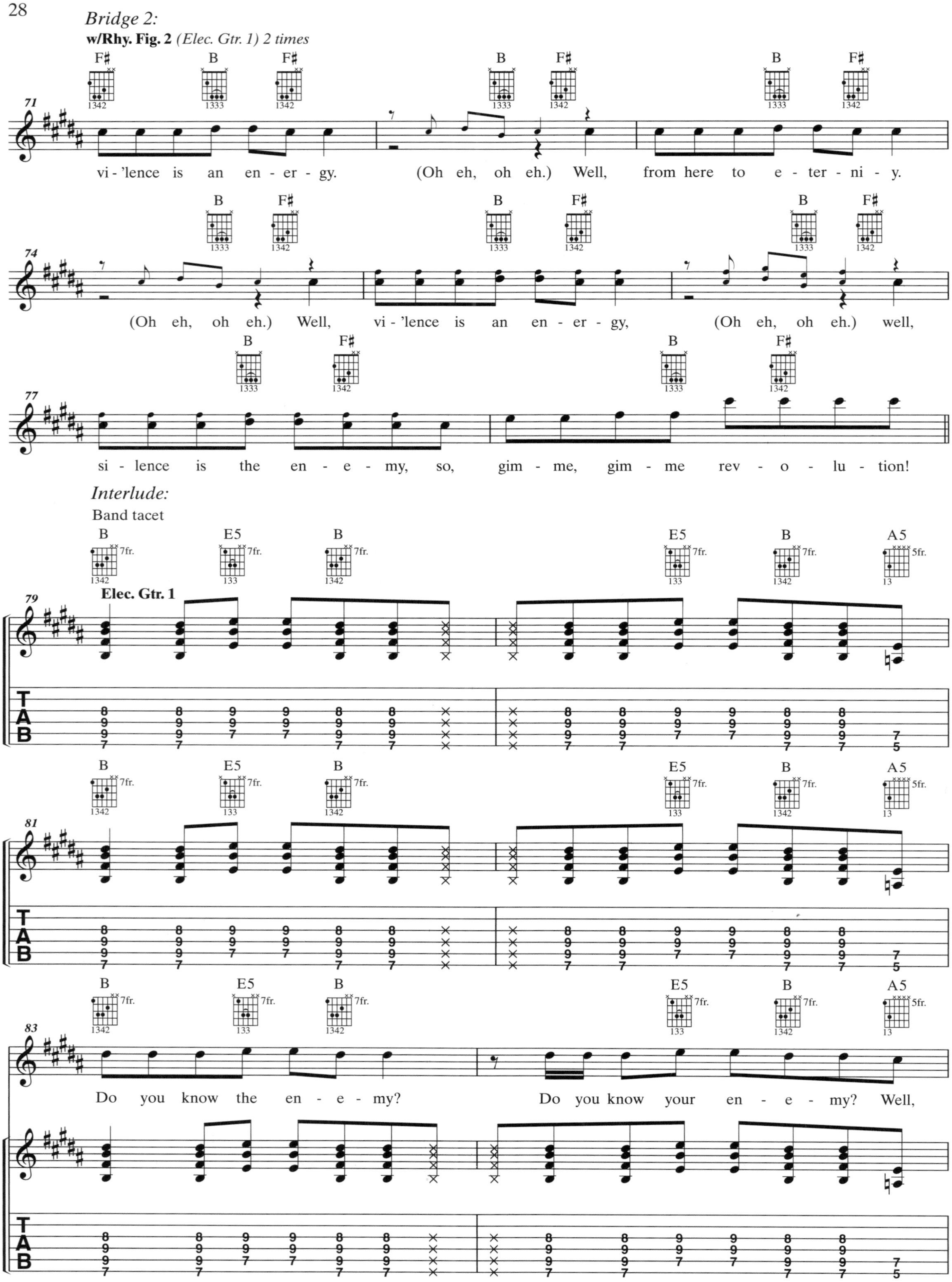

Bridge 2:

w/Rhy. Fig. 2 *(Elec. Gtr. 1) 2 times*

F♯ B F♯ B F♯ B F♯

vi - 'lence is an en - er - gy. (Oh eh, oh eh.) Well, from here to e - ter - ni - y.

B F♯ B F♯ B F♯

(Oh eh, oh eh.) Well, vi - 'lence is an en - er - gy, (Oh eh, oh eh.) well,

B F♯ B F♯

si - lence is the en - e - my, so, gim - me, gim - me rev - o - lu - tion!

Interlude:

Band tacet

B E5 B E5 B A5

Elec. Gtr. 1

B E5 B E5 B A5

B E5 B E5 B A5

Do you know the en - e - my? Do you know your en - e - my? Well,

Band enters
B
E5
B
F♯
7fr.
5fr.
1342
133
13
85
got - ta know the en - e - my. (Rah eh!)
*Elec. Gtr. 1 dbld.
Chorus:
w/Rhy. Fig. 1 (Elec. Gtr. 1) 2 times
A5
87
Do you know the en - e - my? Do you know your en - e - my? Well,
89
got - ta know the en - e - my. (Rah eh!)
91
Do you know the en - e - my? Do you know your en - e - my? Well,
93
got - ta know the en - e - my. (Rah eh!)

Verse 3:
w/Rhy. Fig. 1 (Elec. Gtr. 1) 2 times
B
E5
A5
F♯
7fr.
5fr.
O - ver - throw the ef - fi - gy, the vast ma - jor - i - ty, well, burn - ing down the fore - man of con -
trol. (Oh eh, oh eh.) Si - lence is the en - e - my, a - gainst your ur - gen - cy, so
ral - ly up the de - mons of your soul. (Oh eh, oh eh.)
Elec. Gtr. 2
Elec. Gtr. 1

¡VIVA LA GLORIA!

Lyrics by BILLIE JOE
Music by GREEN DAY

C♯m G♯m A E E/D♯
Say your prayers and light a fire. We're gon-na start a war.
C♯m G♯m A B
Your slo-gan's a gun for hire. It's what we've wait - ed for.
E G♯m A
Hey, Glo-ri - a, this is why we're on the edge.
E G♯m A
The fight of our lives been drawn to this un - dy - ing love.
E
Faster ♩ = 152
N.C.
(cymbals)
Band enters
Chorus:
E G♯m
Elec. Gtr. 2 (w/light dist.)
mf
1. Glo - ri - a, vi - va la Glo - ri - a.
2. Glo - ri - a, where are you, Glo - ri - a?
C♯m A
You blast your name in graf - fi - ti on the walls.
Don't lose your faith to your lost na - i - ve - té.

Am
5fr.
134111
E
231
B
1333
C♯m
4fr.
13421
48
Fall - ing through bro - ken glass_ that's slash - ing through your spir - it.
(Ooh.)
Weath - er the storm__ and don't_ look back on last No - vem - ber,
A
5fr.
134211
B
7fr.
134211
52
I can hear it like__ a jilt - ed crowd.
when your ban - ners__ were burn - ing down.
E
7fr.
1333
G♯m
4fr.
134111
56
Cont. rhy. simile
Glo - ri - a,______ where are___ you,___ Glo - ri - a?
Glo - ri - a,______ vi - va___ la___ Glo - ri - a.
C♯m
4fr.
13421
A
5fr.
134211
60
You found a home__ in all__ your scars and am - mu - ni - tion.
Send me your am - nes - ty__ down to the bro - ken heart - ed.
Am
5fr.
134111
E
231
B
1333
C♯m
4fr.
13421
64
You made your bed__ in sal - ad days a - mongst the ru - ins.
(Ooh.)
Bring us the sea - son that__ we al - ways will re - mem - ber.
To Coda
A
5fr.
134211
B
7fr.
134211
68
Ash - es to ash - es of______ our youth,
Don't let the bon - fires go

Verse:
E
7fr.
1333
G♯m
4fr.
134111
C♯m
4fr.
13421
Elec. Gtr. 2
72
She smashed her knuck - les in - to win - ter.
(Glo - ri -
A
5fr.
134211
E
7fr.
1333
B
7fr.
134211
Cont. rhy. simile
76
As au-tumn's wind fades in - to black.
a.)
E
7fr.
1333
G♯m
4fr.
134111
C♯m
4fr.
13421
80
She is the saint of all the sin - ners,
(Glo - ri -
A
5fr.
134211
E
231
B
7fr.
134211
Elec. Gtr. 2
12 fr
⑥
84
the one that's fall - en through the cracks.
a.)
So don't
A
5fr.
134211
B
7fr.
134211
D.S. 𝄋 al Coda
88
put a - way your burn - ing light.
Elec. Gtr. 3 (w/light dist.)
mf
T
A
B
5 2 5
4 5 7
0 0 0

Coda
B
7fr.
134211
92
A
111
E
231
out.
So, Glo - ri - a,
Elec. Gtr. 3
Elec. Gtr. 2
96
A
111
E
231
send out your mes-sage of
the light that shad-ows in the night.

B
Bsus
2fr.
B
A
E
1333
1334
1333
111
231
100
Glo - ri - a,
A
E
A
111
231
111
104
where's your un - dy - ing love?
Tell me the

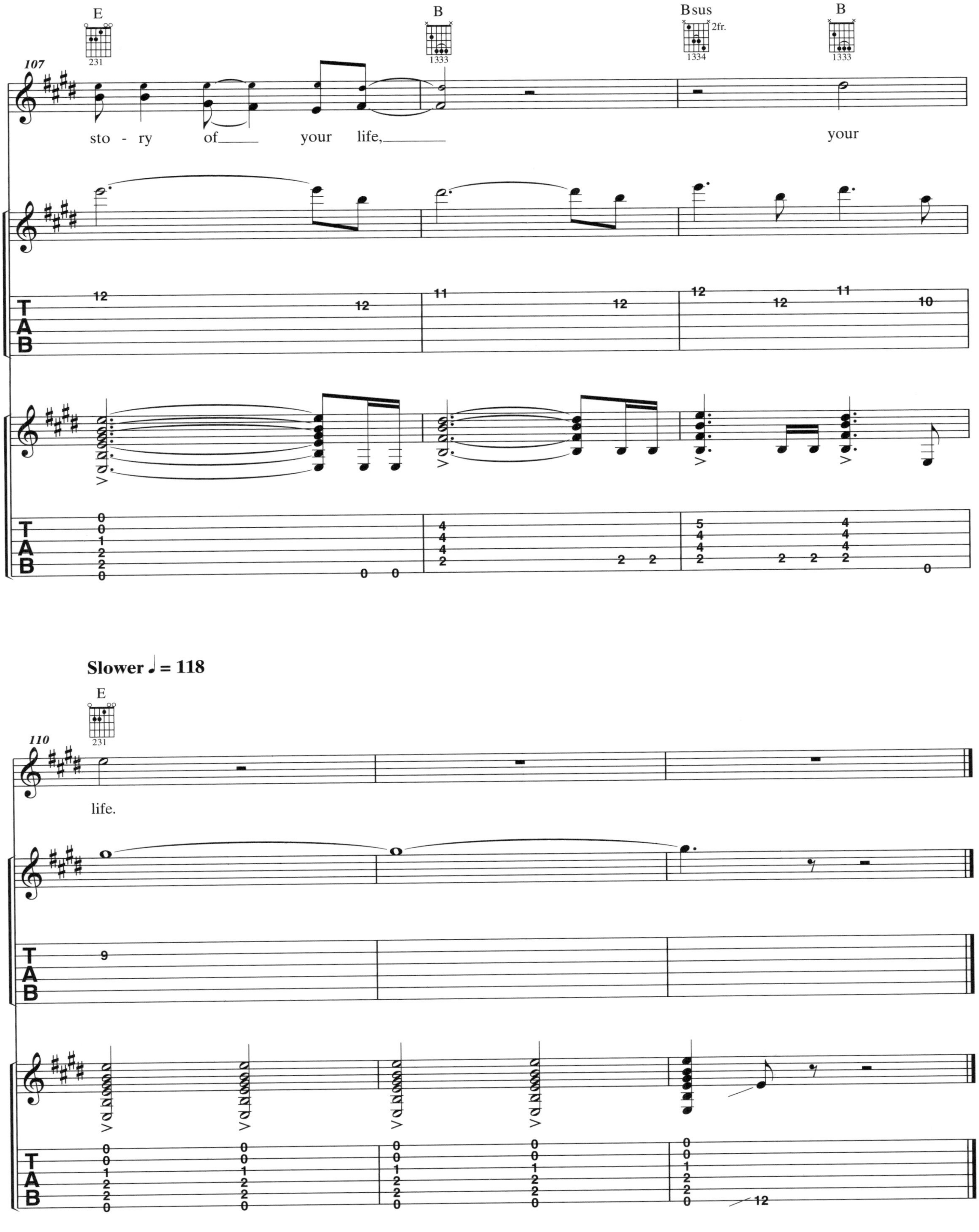

E B Bsus B

107

sto - ry of your life, your

Slower ♩ = 118

E

110

life.

BEFORE THE LOBOTOMY

Lyrics by BILLIE JOE
Music by GREEN DAY

Dm(9)/F
C
1.
E♭
2.
E♭
4fr.
when the rain had washed_ a - way_ all these scat-tered dreams._
Songs of yes - ter-day____ now live_ in the un-der - ground._
Interlude:
D5 G5 A5
Elec. Gtr. 1 (w/light dist.)
mf
Elec. Gtr. 2 (w/light dist.)
f
Band enters
N.C.
5fr.
3fr.
Elec. Gtr. 2
(Ooh.
)

Verses 3 & 4:

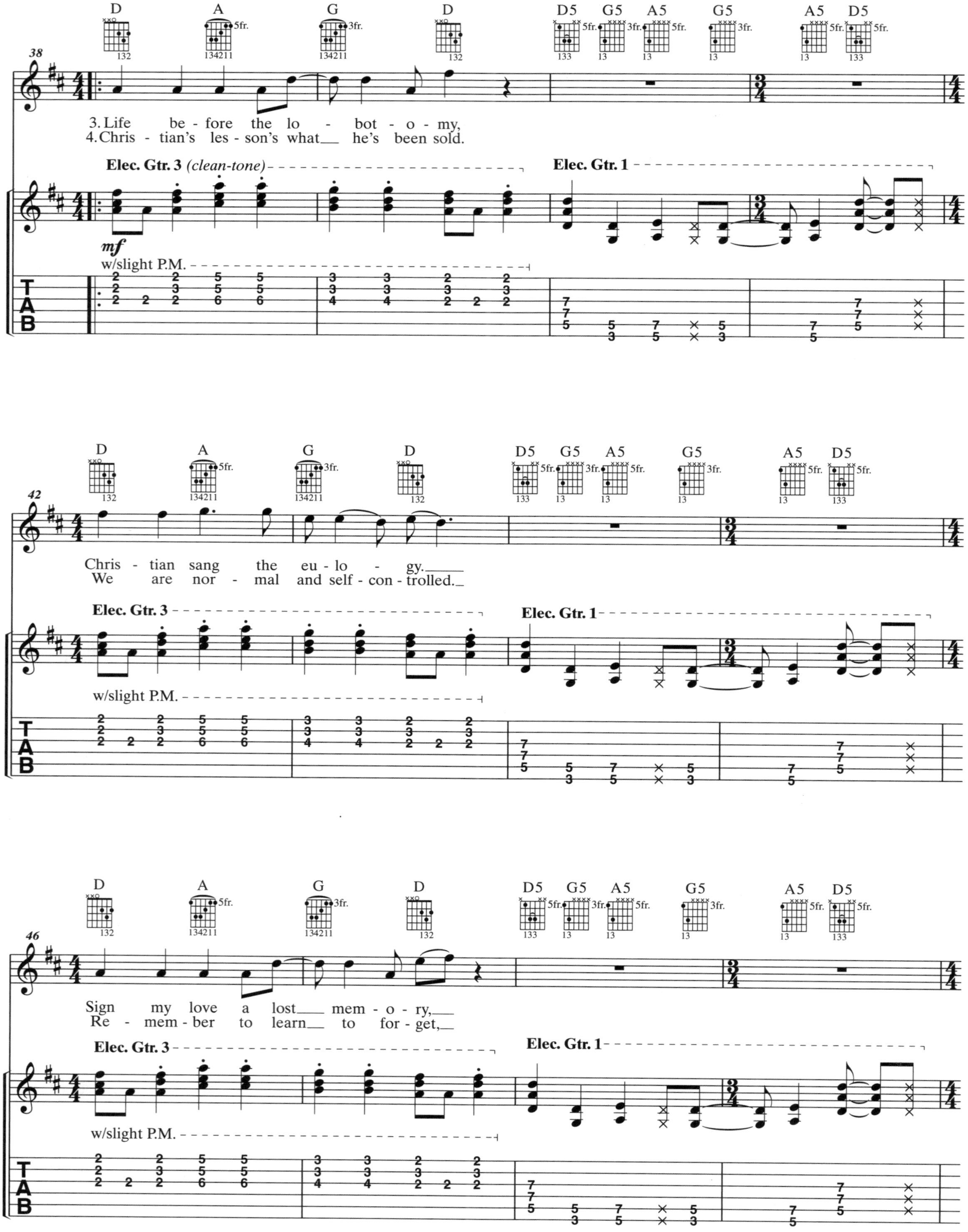

D A G D D5 G5 A5 G5 A5 D5

38

3. Life be - fore the lo - bot - o - my,
4. Chris - tian's les - son's what__ he's been sold.

Elec. Gtr. 3 *(clean-tone)* **Elec. Gtr. 1**

mf

w/slight P.M.

D A G D D5 G5 A5 G5 A5 D5

42

Chris - tian sang the eu - lo - gy.____
We are nor - mal and self - con - trolled._

Elec. Gtr. 3 **Elec. Gtr. 1**

w/slight P.M.

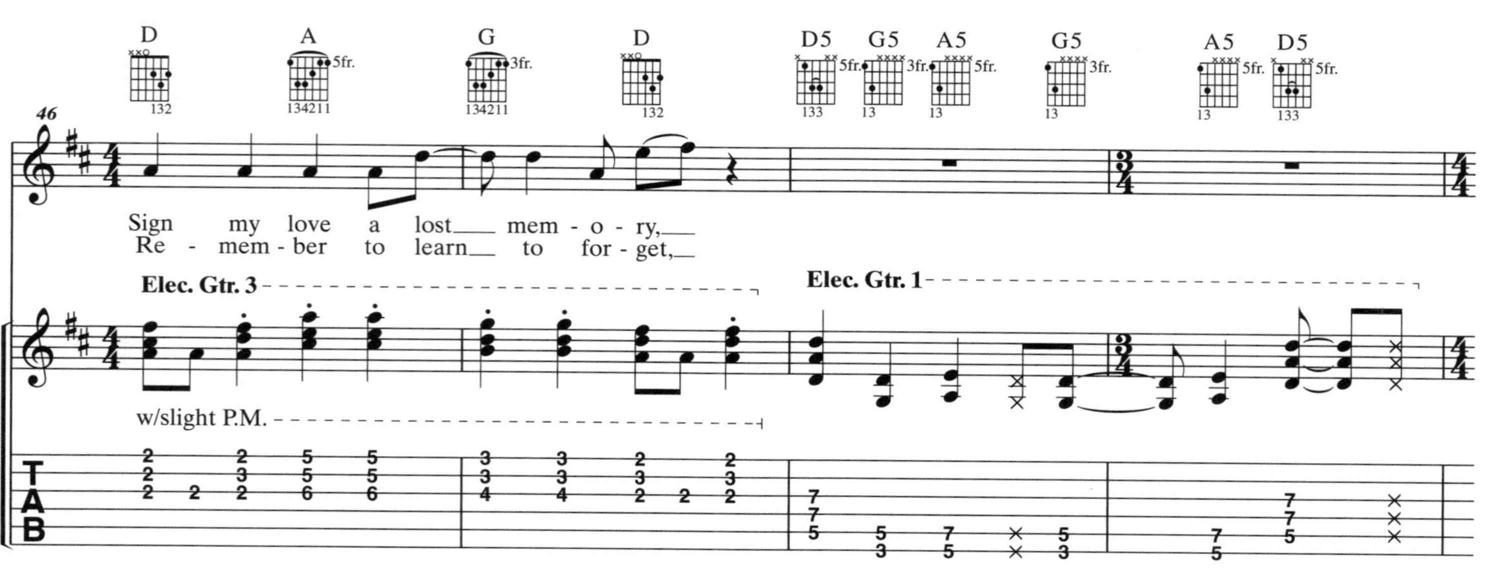

D
A
G
D
D5
G5
A5
G5
A5
D5
50
from the end of the___ cen - tu - ry.___
whis - key shots and cheap_ cig - a - rettes._
Well,
Well,
Elec. Gtr. 3
Elec. Gtr. 1
w/slight P.M.
(1st time only)
Elec. Gtr. 1
(2nd time only)
Elec. Gtr. 2
54
it's e - nough to make___ you sick,_ to cast a stone and throw___ a brick._ But
I'm not stoned, I'm just___ fucked up.___ I got so high, I can't___ stand up.___ Well,
Elec. Gtr. 1
58
when the sky is fall - ing down,_ it burned your dreams in - to___
I'm not cursed, 'cause I've___ been blessed._ I'm not in love, 'cause I'm___

1.
2.
D5
A5
5fr.
61
the ground.
a
mess.
Like
Cont. in slashes
Elec. Gtr. 2
Bridge:
D
A
Elec. Gtr. 1
Cont. rhy. simile
65
ref - u - gees,
we're lost like ref - u - gees.
Like
69
ref - u - gees,
we're lost like ref - u - gees.
The bru -
C
G
3fr.
E♭
B♭
6fr.
73
tal - i - ty
of re - al - i - ty
is the
(Ah,
ah,
Elec. Gtr. 3
hold
hold

D
D5
free - dom that keeps me from...
ah.)
Elec. Gtr. 2
hold
Elec. Gtr. 1
P.M.
Verses 5 & 6:
G
D(9)/F♯
5. Dream - ing, I was on - ly dream - ing
6. Dy - ing, ev - 'ry - one's re - mind - ed.
Rhy. Fig. 1B
Elec. Gtr. 2
Rhy. Fig. 1A
Elec. Gtr. 3
hold throughout
Rhy. Fig. 1
Elec. Gtr. 1

Dm(9)/F
C
E♭
85
of an - oth - er place and time, where my fam-'ly's from.
Hearts are washed in mis - er - y, drenched in gas - o - line.
end Rhy. Fig. 1B
end Rhy. Fig. 1A
end Rhy. Fig. 1
w/Rhy. Figs. 1 (Elec. Gtr. 1), 1A (Elec. Gtr. 3), & 1B (Elec. Gtr. 2)
G
D(9)/F♯
Dm(9)/F
89
Sing - ing, I can hear them sing - ing, when the rain had washed
Laugh - ter, there is no more laugh - ter. Songs of yes - ter - day
1.
2.
Band tacet
C
E♭
C
Cm
94
a - way all these scat-tered dreams. in the un-der - ground.
now live
Elec. Gtr. 4 (clean-tone w/chorus & delay)
mp
fingerstyle

CHRISTIAN'S INFERNO

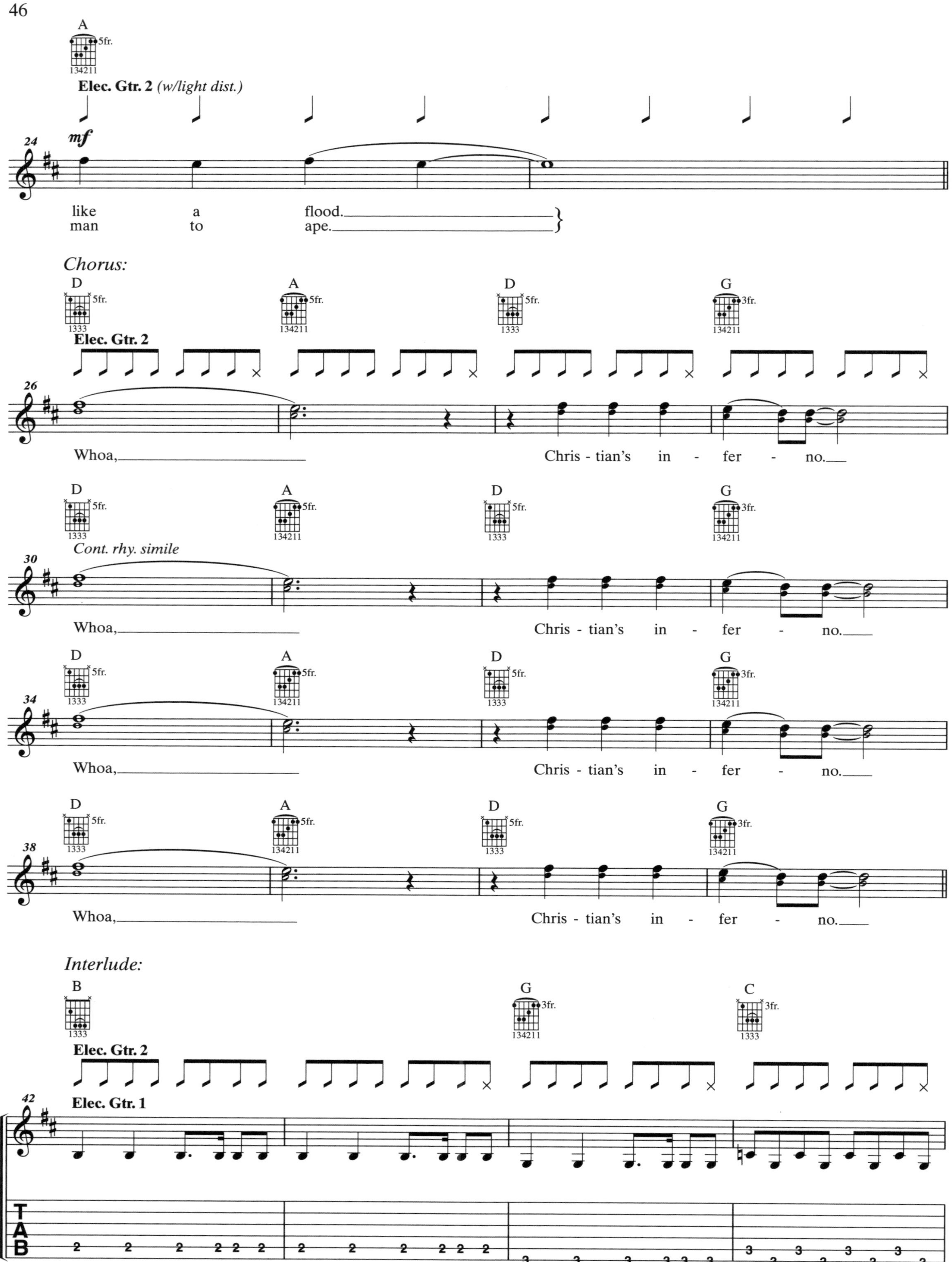
A
5fr.
134211
Elec. Gtr. 2 (w/light dist.)
mf
like a flood.
man to ape.
Chorus:
D A D G
5fr. 5fr. 5fr. 3fr.
1333 134211 1333 134211
Elec. Gtr. 2
Whoa, Chris - tian's in - fer - no.
Cont. rhy. simile
Whoa, Chris - tian's in - fer - no.
Whoa, Chris - tian's in - fer - no.
Whoa, Chris - tian's in - fer - no.
Interlude:
B G C
1333 134211 1333
3fr. 3fr.
Elec. Gtr. 2
Elec. Gtr. 1
T
A
B
2 2 2 2 2 2
2 2 2 2 2 2
3 3 3 3 3 3
3 3 3 3 3 3 3 3

1.
D.S. 𝄋
2.
B
1333
G
3fr.
134211
C
3fr.
1333
C
3fr.
1333
46
2 2 2 2 2 2
2 2 2 2 2 2
3 3 3 3 3 3
3 3 3 3 3 3 3 3
3 3 3 3 3 3 3 3
Elec. Gtr. 3 (w/light dist.)
mf
14
Instrumental:
1.2.3.
4.
B
7fr.
1342
E
7fr.
1333
C
8fr.
1342
F
8fr.
1333
B
7fr.
1342
B
7fr.
1342
Elec. Gtr. 2
Elec. Gtr. 4 (w/light dist.)
51
mf
grad. bend
1 1/2
12 11 12 11
12 11 11 12 11
13 12 13 15
12 11 11 12 11
12
Elec. Gtr. 3
19
Chorus:
D
5fr.
1333
A
5fr.
134211
D
5fr.
1333
G
3fr.
134211
Elec. Gtr. 2 resume chorus fig. simile
56
Whoa,
Chris - tian's in - fer - no.

D
A
D
G
5fr.
3fr.
1333
134211
60
Whoa,
Chris - tian's in - fer - no.
64
Whoa,
Chris - tian's in - fer - no.
68
Whoa,
Chris - tian's in -
Outro:
G
F/G
10fr.
1111
Elec. Gtr. 2
71
fer - no.
75
79
B5
7fr.
134
*w/delay.

LAST NIGHT ON EARTH

Lyrics by BILLIE JOE
Music by GREEN DAY

D
Dm
A
Send - ing all my love to you.
I'm send - ing all my love to you.
A+
A6
A7
2fr.
You are the moon - light of my life ev - 'ry night.
So if you dare to sec - ond guess, you could rest
D
Dm
A
Giv - ing all my love to you.
as - sured that all my love's for you.
Chorus:
D
Dm
A
Acous. Gtr. cont. rhy. simile
My beat - ing heart be - longs to you.
Elec. Gtr. 1
hold throughout
(2nd time only)

D
Dm
A
15
I walked for miles 'til I found you.
D
Dm
A
A/G
A/F♯
A/E
17
I'm here to hon-or you. If I lose ev-'ry-thing in the fire,
1.
D
Dm
A
A+
A6
A7
Acous. Gtr.
Acous. Gtr. resume rhy. fig. simile
19
I'm send-ing all my love to you.
Elec. Gtr. 2 (clean-tone w/heavy delay)
mf

D.S. 𝄋
2.
D
Dm
A
132
231
111
I'm send-ing all my love_ to you._
Elec. Gtr. 2
w/slide
Elec. Gtr. 1
Acous. Gtr. & Elec. Gtr. 1
Instrumental:
A
A+
A6
A7
2fr.
211
311
411
Acous. Gtr. & Elec. Gtr. 1 resume chorus fig. simile

Chorus:
D
Dm
A
Elec. Gtr. 1 resume chorus fig. simile
Acous. Gtr. cont. rhy. simile
My beat - ing heart be - longs to you.
I walked for miles 'til I found you.
I'm here to hon-or you.
A
A/G
A/F♯
A/E
Acous. Gtr. & Elec. Gtr. 1
If I lose ev - 'ry-thing in the fire, did I ev-er make it through?
Outro:
Band tacet
A+
A6
A7
2fr.
Piano
hold throughout
rit.

EAST JESUS NOWHERE

Lyrics by BILLIE JOE
Music by GREEN DAY

Moderately fast shuffle ♩ = 138

16
D5 A5 E5 D5 A5
su - i - cide, like a dog that's been sod - om - ized. Well,
19
E5 G5 E5 D5 E5 G5 E5 D5
stand up! All the white boys. Sit down!
22
E5 G5 E5 D5 E5
And the black girls. Stand up! You're the sol - diers.
25
G5 E5 D5 E5 D5 A5
Sit down! of the new world.
Pre-chorus:
B5
1. Put your faith in a
2. See additional lyrics

28
D5 A5 B5 D5 A5
mir - a - cle and it's non - de - nom - i - na - tion - al.
T
A
B
31
B5 D5 A5 B5
Join the choir, we'll be sing - ing in the church of
T
A
B
A
5fr.
134211
Elec. Gtr. 1
3 3 3
Cont. in notation
Chorus:
34
E G
wish - ful think - ing.
A fire burns to - day of
Elec. Gtr. 2
Elec. Gtrs. 1 & 2
f
T
A
B
37
A C5 B5 E
blas - phe - my and gen - o - cide. The si - rens of de - cay
T
A
B

To Coda 

G
A
C5
D5
will in - fil - trate the faith fa - nat - ics.
Guitar Solo:
w/Rhy. Fig. 1 (Elec. Gtr. 2)
1.
2.
E5 G5 E5 D5
E5
G5 E5 D5
E5
(E5)
D5 A5
Elec. Gtr. 1
Bridge:
Gtrs. tacet
N.C. (E5)
(G5)
(B5)
mf
Oh, bless me, Lord, for I have sinned.
(E5)
(G5)
(B5)
It's been a life - time since I last con - fessed.
(E5)
(G5)
I threw my crutch - es in the riv -
(B5)
(E5)
- er of a shad - ow of doubt. And I'll be dressed
D.S. 𝄋 al Coda
D5
A5
5fr.
133
(G5)
(B5)
Elec. Gtr. 1
up in my Sun - day best.

Coda
E5
G5
E5
D5
E5
G5
E5
D5
7fr.
10fr.
5fr.
133
Elec. Gtr. 1
Elec. Gtr. 2
trem. pick
1.
2.
Cont. in notation
Elec. Gtrs. 1 & 2
(whispered) Don't test me.
Sec - ond guess me.
Pro - test me. You will

Pre-chorus:
D5 A5 B5 D5 A5
dis - ap - pear. I want to know who's al - lowed to breed:
mf
B5 D5 A5 B5
All the dogs who nev - er learned to read, mis - sion - ar - y pol - i -
D5 A5 B5 D5
ti - cians, and the cops of the new re - li - gion.
Cont. in slashes
Instrumental Chorus:
E5 G5 A5 C5 B5
3fr. 5fr. 3fr.
Elec. Gtr. 1
f
Elec. Gtr. 2
f

E5
7fr.
133
G5
3fr.
133
A5
5fr.
133
C5
3fr.
133
D5
5fr.
133
Cont. in notation
89
93
E5
F5
E5
mf
divisi (high E, 1st time only)
trem. pick
Elec. Gtr. 1
mf
1/2
97
F5
E5
1.
2.
A
mp
1/2

Say a prayer for the family.
Drop a coin for humanity.
Ain't this uniform flattering?
I never asked you a goddamn thing.
(To Chorus:)

PEACEMAKER

Lyrics by BILLIE JOE
Music by GREEN DAY

15
call of the ban - shee, hey hey, hey hey hey hey hey. As
call up the cap - tain, hey, hey, hey, hey, hey, hey, hey. Well,
To Coda
Bm
13421
19
God as my wit - ness, the in - fi - dels are gon - na pay. 2. Well,
death to the lov - er that you were dream - ing of. 4. Well,
Verses 2 & 4:
Bm
13421
Acous. Gtr. & Elec. Gtr. 1 cont. rhy. simile
23
call the as - sas - sin, the or - gasm, a spasm of love and hate. For
this is a stand - off, a Mol - o - tov cock - tail on the house. You
F♯
134211
27
what will di - vide us? The right - eous and the meek. Well,
thought I was a write - off, you bet - ter think a - gain. Well,
31
call of the wild, hey hey, hey hey hey hey hey. Well,
call the peace - mak - er. hey, hey, hey, hey, hey, hey, hey. I'm

Bm
35
death to the girl at the end of the ser - e - nade.
gon-na send you back to the place where it all be - gan.
Ven -
Elec. Gtr. 3 (clean-tone)
mf
Chorus:
F♯
39
Acous. Gtr. & Elec. Gtr. 1 cont. rhy. simile
det - ta, sweet ven - det - ta, this Ber -
Rhy. Fig. 1
Bm
43
et - ta of the night. This
1/2
Em
Bm
47
fire and the de - sire. Well,

1.
F♯
Bm
shots ring-ing out on the ho - ly par - a - site.
3. Well,
end Rhy. Fig. 1
2.
Bm
Freely
Band tacet
Acous. Gtr. & Elec. Gtr. 1
Elec. Gtr. 4 (w/dist.)
mf
rake
a tempo
Instrumental:
w/Rhy. Fig. 1 (Elec. Gtr. 3)
F♯
Acous. Gtr. & Elec. Gtr. 1 resume rhy. fig. simile
Elec. Gtr. 5 (w/dist.)
mf
Elec. Gtr. 4

Bm
13421
Em
23
Bm
13421
F♯
134211
Bm
13421
D.S. 𝄋 al Coda
5. Well,

Coda
F♯
134211
74
Well, death to the ones at the end of the ser - en - ade.
Elec. Gtr. 2
Elec. Gtr. 3

Bm
13421
F♯
134211
77
Well, death to the ones at the end of the ser - en - ade.

Verse 5:
Well, now the caretakers, the undertakers
Saw I'm gonna go out and get a peacemaker.
This is a neo-Saint Valentines massacre.
Well, call up the Gaza, hey, hey, hey, hey, hey, hey, hey.
Well, death to the ones at the end of the serenade.
(To Coda)

LAST OF THE AMERICAN GIRLS

Lyrics by BILLIE JOE
Music by GREEN DAY

B
7fr.
134211
E
7fr.
1333
11
par - a - noid, en-dan-gered spe-cies head-ed in-to ex-tinc - tion. She is
2 2 2 2 2 2 2 2 2 2 2 2 2 2 2 2 7 7 7 7 7 7 7 7 7 7 7 7 7 7 7 0
B
F♯
B
15
one of a kind. Well, she's the last of the A-mer-i-can girls. 2. She wears her
2 2 2 2 2 2 2 2 9 9 9 9 9 9 9 0 2 2 2 2 2 2 2 2 2 2 2 2 2
Verses 2 & 3:
B
E
19
o-ver - coat for the com-ing of the nu-clear win - ter. She is
(3.) vi-nyl rec - ords, sing-ing songs on the eve of de-struc - tion. She's a
Rhy. Fig. 1
Elec. Gtr. 1 (w/light dist.)
mf
2 2 2 2 2 2 2 2 2 2 2 2 2 2 2 2 0 0 0 0 0 0 0 0 0 0 0 0 0 0 0 0
Fill 1
Elec. Gtr. 2 (w/light dist.)
mf
7 7 7 7 7 7 7 7 7 6 7 9 9
Rhy. Fig. 1A
Elec. Gtr. 3 (clean-tone)
mf
(2nd time only)

B
7fr.
134211
F♯
134211
23
rid - ing her bike like a fu - gi - tive of crit - i - cal mass.
She's on a
suck - er for all the crim - i - nals break - ing the laws.
She will
end Rhy. Fig. 1
end Rhy. Fig. 1A
Elec. Gtr. 4 (clean-tone)
mp
(2nd time only)
w/Rhy. Fig. 1 (Elec. Gtr. 1)
w/Rhy. Fig. 1A (Elec. Gtr. 3) 2nd time only
w/Fill 1 (Elec. Gtr. 2)
B
7fr.
134211
E
7fr.
1333
27
hun - ger strike for the ones who won't make it for din - ner.
She makes e -
come in first for the end of west - ern civ - il - i - za - tion.
She's the

B
F♯
nough to sur - vive__ for a hol - i - day of work - ing class.__ She's a
end-less war,__ she's a he - ro for the lost__ cause.__ Like a
hold
Chorus:
B
B7
E
Em
Elec. Gtr. 1
run-a - way__ of the es - tab-lish-ment in-cor - por-a - ted. She won't co-
hur-ri - cane__ in the heart of the dev - as-ta - tion. She's a-
Elec. Gtr. 5 (w/light dist.)
mf
op - er - ate.__ Well, she's the last of the A-mer-i-can girls.__
nat-'ral dis - as - ter. She's the last of the A-mer-i-can girls.__
Elec. Gtr. 6 (w/dist.)
mf

1.
2.
B
E
7fr.
134211
1333
42
3. She plays her
Elec. Gtr. 5
Guitar Solo:
Elec. Gtr. 1
46
Elec. Gtr. 7 (w/light dist.)
mf

B
7fr.
134211
F♯
134211
1.
2.
50
She puts her
1
(4)
Chorus:
B7
131211
E
1333
Em
13421
55
Elec. Gtr. 1 resume chorus fig. simile
make-up on like graf - fi - ti on the walls of the heart - land.
She's got her
Elec. Gtr. 5
59
lit - tle book of con - spir - a - cies right in her hand.
She will
63
come in first for the end of west - ern civ - il - i - za - tion.
She's a

B
F♯
E
7fr.
134211
1333
Elec. Gtr. 1
Elec. Gtr. 6
Cont. rhy. simile
nat-'ral dis-as - ter. She's the last of the A-mer-i-can girls.
Oh yeah.
All right.
Oh yeah.

MURDER CITY

Lyrics by BILLIE JOE
Music by GREEN DAY

Verse:
B5
D♯5
G♯5
E5
F♯5
1. I'm wide a - wake after the ri - ots.
2. Chris-tians cry - ing in the bath - room
This dem-on - stra - tion of our an - guish.
and I just want to bum a cig - a - rette.
This em-pty laugh - ter has no rea - son,
We've come so far, we've been so wast - ed.
Elec. Gtr. 1
P.M.

E5
7fr.
133
B5
7fr.
134
F♯5
9fr.
133
like a bot-tle of your fa - v'rite poi - son.
It's writ-ten all o - ver our fac - es.
P.M.
P.M.
P.M.
To Coda
E
7fr.
1333
Em
7fr.
1342
We are the last call and we're so pa - thet - ic.
Chorus:
B
7fr.
1342
D♯
6fr.
1333
Elec. Gtr. 1 resume chorus fig. simile
Des - per - ate, but not hope - less.
G♯5
4fr.
134
E
7fr.
1333
Em
7fr.
1342
I feel so use - less in the mur - der cit - y.
B
7fr.
1342
D♯
6fr.
1333
Des - per - ate, but not help - less.

G♯5
E
Em
The clock strikes mid - night in the mur - der cit - y.

Guitar Solo:

B
D♯
Elec. Gtr. 1 resume chorus fig. simile
Riff A
Elec. Gtr. 2 (w/light dist.)
mf

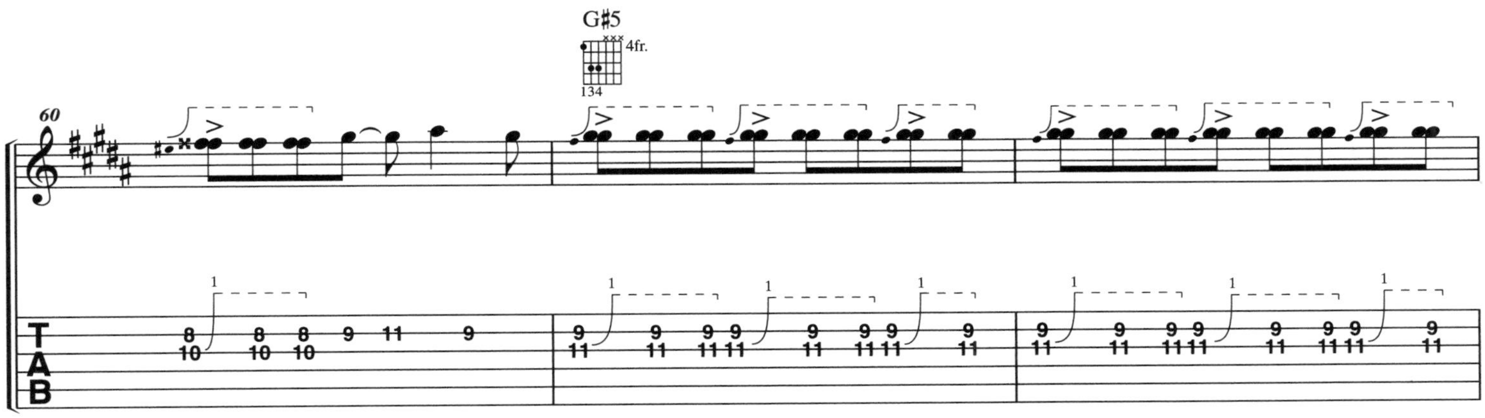
G♯5

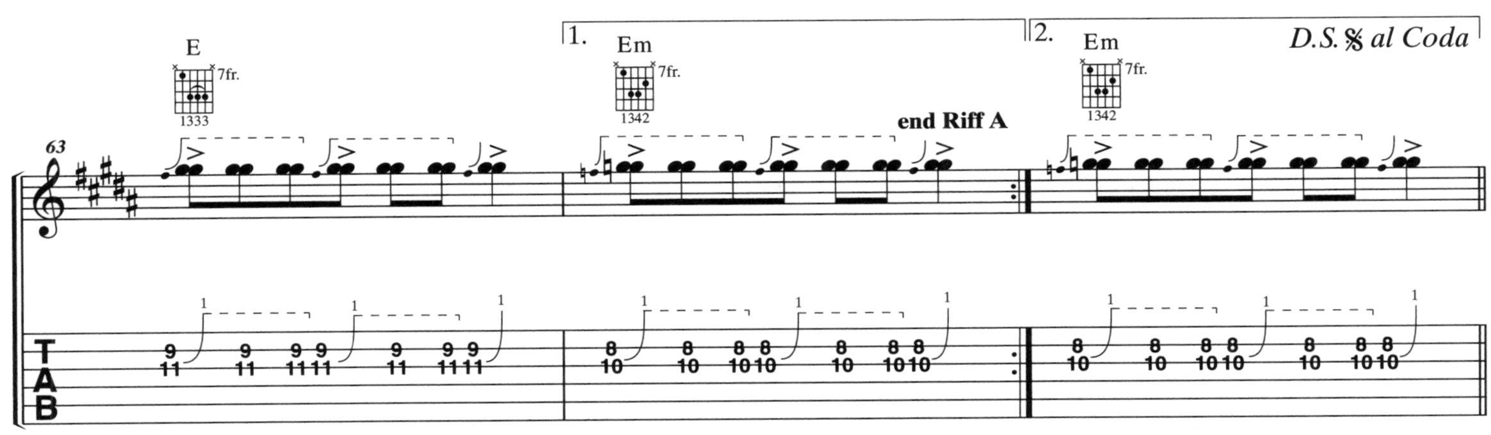
E
1. Em
end Riff A
2. Em
D.S. 𝄋 al Coda

Coda
Em
7fr.
1342
Drums
so pa - thet - ic.
Chorus:
w/Riff A (Elec. Gtr. 2) 2nd time only
B
7fr.
1342
D♯
6fr.
1333
Elec. Gtr. 1 resume chorus fig. simile
Des - per - ate, but not hope - less.
G♯5
4fr.
134
E
7fr.
1333
Em
7fr.
1342
I feel so use - less in the the mur - der cit - y.
w/Riff A (Elec. Gtr. 2) 1st 6 meas., 2nd time only
B
D♯
Des - per - ate, but not help - less.
G♯5
1.
E
Em
2.
E
Elec. Gtr. 1
The clock strikes mid - night in the mur - der cit - y.
Elec. Gtr. 2

¿VIVA LA GLORIA? (LITTLE GIRL)

Lyrics by BILLIE JOE
Music by GREEN DAY

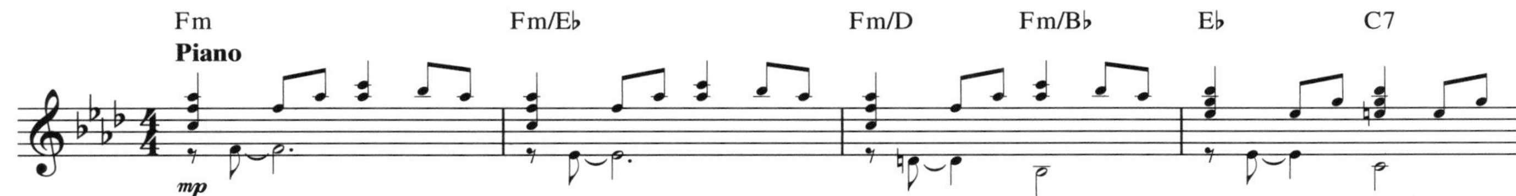

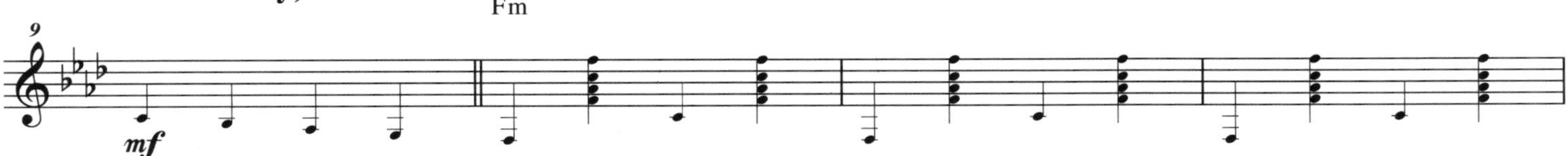

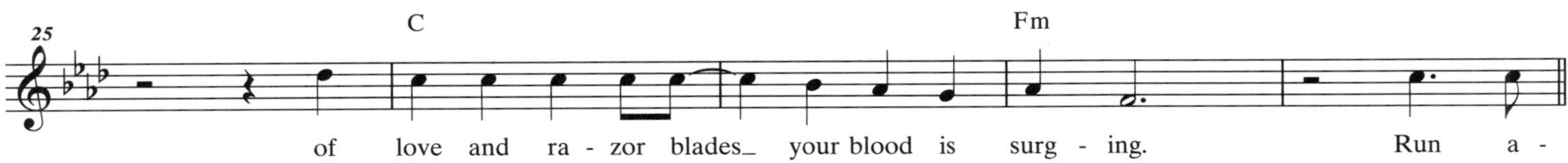

Chorus:
30
F5
D♭5
way from the riv - er to the street and
Elec. Gtr. 1 (dbld. by 2nd gtr.)
TAB
34
C5
F5
find your - self with your face in the gut - ter. You're a
38
D♭5
stray for the Sal - va - tion Ar - my. There
42
C5
is no place like home when you got no place to

46
Fm
To Coda
go.
Lit - tle
Elec. Gtr. 1 cont. in slashes
Elec. Gtr. 2 (clean-tone w/reverb)
mf
fast vibrato w/trem. bar
Verse 2:
Fm
8fr.
134111
D♭
4fr.
1333
Elec. Gtr. 1
50
girl, lit - tle girl, your life is call - ing the
C
3fr.
1333
Fm
8fr.
134111
54
char - la - tans and saints of your a - ban - don. Lit - tle
Elec. Gtr. 2
fast vibrato w/trem. bar
w/trem. bar
-1/2

D♭
4fr.
1333
58
one, lit - tle one, the sky is fall - ing. Your
fast vibrato w/trem. bar
fast vibrato w/trem. bar
C
3fr.
1333
Fm
8fr.
134111
62
life - boat of de - cep - tion is now sail - ing. In the
-1/2
w/trem. bar
fast vibrato w/trem. bar
-1/2
D♭
4fr.
1333
66
wake all the way no rhyme or rea - son, your
w/trem. bar

C 3fr. 1333 — Fm 8fr. 134111

70

blood - shot eyes will show your heart of trea - son. Lit - tle

w/trem. bar -1/2

T A B: 3 | 6 5 3 3 | 1 -1/2 |

D♭ 4fr. 1333

74

girl, lit - tle girl, you dirt - y li - ar. You're

C 3fr. 1333 — Fm 8fr. 134111

D.S. 𝄋 al Coda

78

just a junk - ie preach - ing to the choir.___ Run a -

fast vibrato w/trem. bar

fast vibrato w/trem. bar

T A B: 8 8 9 | | 8 10 | 9 |

Bridge:

𝄌 *Coda*

D♭ 4fr. 1333 — A♭ 4fr. 134211

82

The trac - es of blood al - ways fol - low you home_

Db (4fr., 1333) Ab (4fr., 134211)

86

— like the mas - car - a tears from your get - a - way.

Db (4fr., 1333) Ab (4fr., 134211)

90

You're walk - ing with blis - ters and run - ning with

Glor - i - a.

C (3fr., 1333)

94

shears. So un - ho - ly sis - ter of grace.

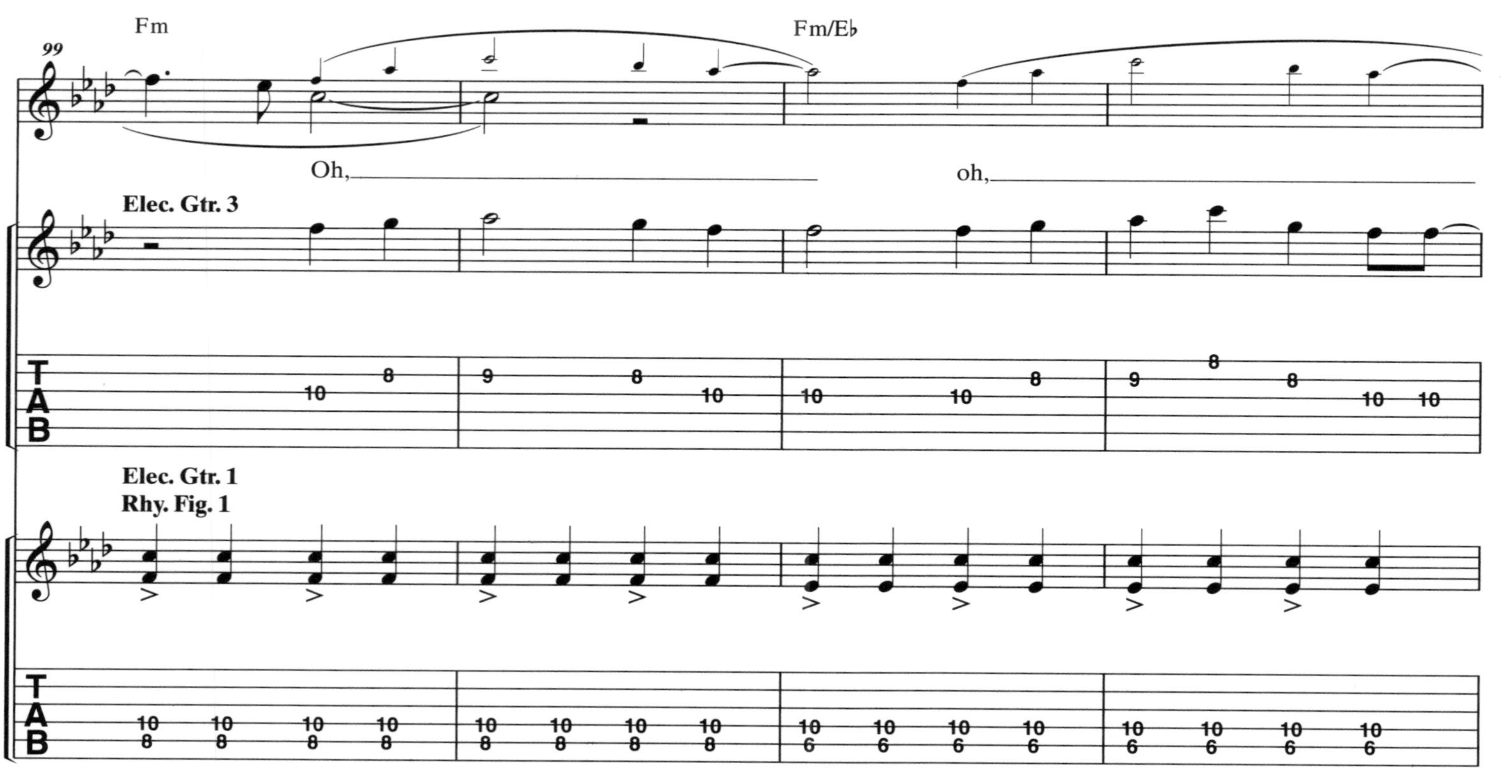

Fm/D
Fm/B♭
E♭
C
103
oh,
oh,
oh.
end Rhy. Fig. 1
w/Rhy. Fig. 1 (Elec. Gtr. 1) cont. simile
Fm
Fm/E♭
Fm/D
107
Oh,
oh,
oh,
1.2.
3.
Fm/B♭
E♭
C
E♭
C
112
oh,
oh.
oh,
Run a -

Chorus:
F5
Db5
way
from the riv - er to the street and
Elec. Gtr. 1
C5
F5
find your - self with your face in the gut - ter. You're a
Db5
stray
from the Sal - va - tion Ar - my. There
C5
is no place like home.
(sfx)

RESTLESS HEART SYNDROME

*Strum pattern for Acous. Gtr.
Acous. Gtr. tacet 8 meas. first time only (enter at meas. 13)
Second time, play through entire verse.

Am
Am/G
D/F♯
F
It's got me beg - ging on my hands and knees. So
for bro - ken hearts and feel - ing in - se - cure. You'd
(2nd time only)
Am
Am/G
Am/F♯
Am/F
Am
Am/G
Piano cont. simile
Elec. Gtr. 1 cont. simile, 2nd time only
take me to e - mer - gen - cy, 'cause some - thing seems to be miss -
be sur - prised what I en - dure. What makes you feel so self - as -
Band enters
D/F♯
F
Am
Am/G
Am/F♯
Am/F
ing. Some - bod - y take the pain a - way.
sured? I need to find a place to hide.
Am
Am/G
D/F♯
Fmaj7
Am
Am/G
It's like an ul - cer bleed - ing in my brain. So send me to the
You nev - er know what could be wait - ing out - side. The ac - ci - dents that
Am/F♯
Am/F
Am
Am/G
D/F♯
Fmaj7
phar - ma - cy, so I can lose my mem - o - ry.
you could find. It's like some kind of su - i - cide.

Pre-chorus:
Dm
Dm/C
Bm7(♭5)
B♭maj7
Acous. Gtr. cont. rhy. simile
I'm e - lat - ed, med - i - cat - ed.
So what ails you is what im - pales you.
Elec. Gtr. 1
hold throughout
(2nd time only)
Lord knows, I tried to find a way to run a - way.
I feel like I've been cru - ci - fied to be sat - is - fied.
1.
2.
E
Acous. Gtr.

Chorus:
Am
Am/G
F♯m7(♭5)
D
Acous. Gtr.
I'm a vic - tim of my symp - tom. I am my own worst en - e - my.
Elec. Gtr. 1
hold throughout
G
E
You're a vic - tim of your symp - tom.
You are your own worst en - e - my. Know your en - e - my.

Guitar Solo:

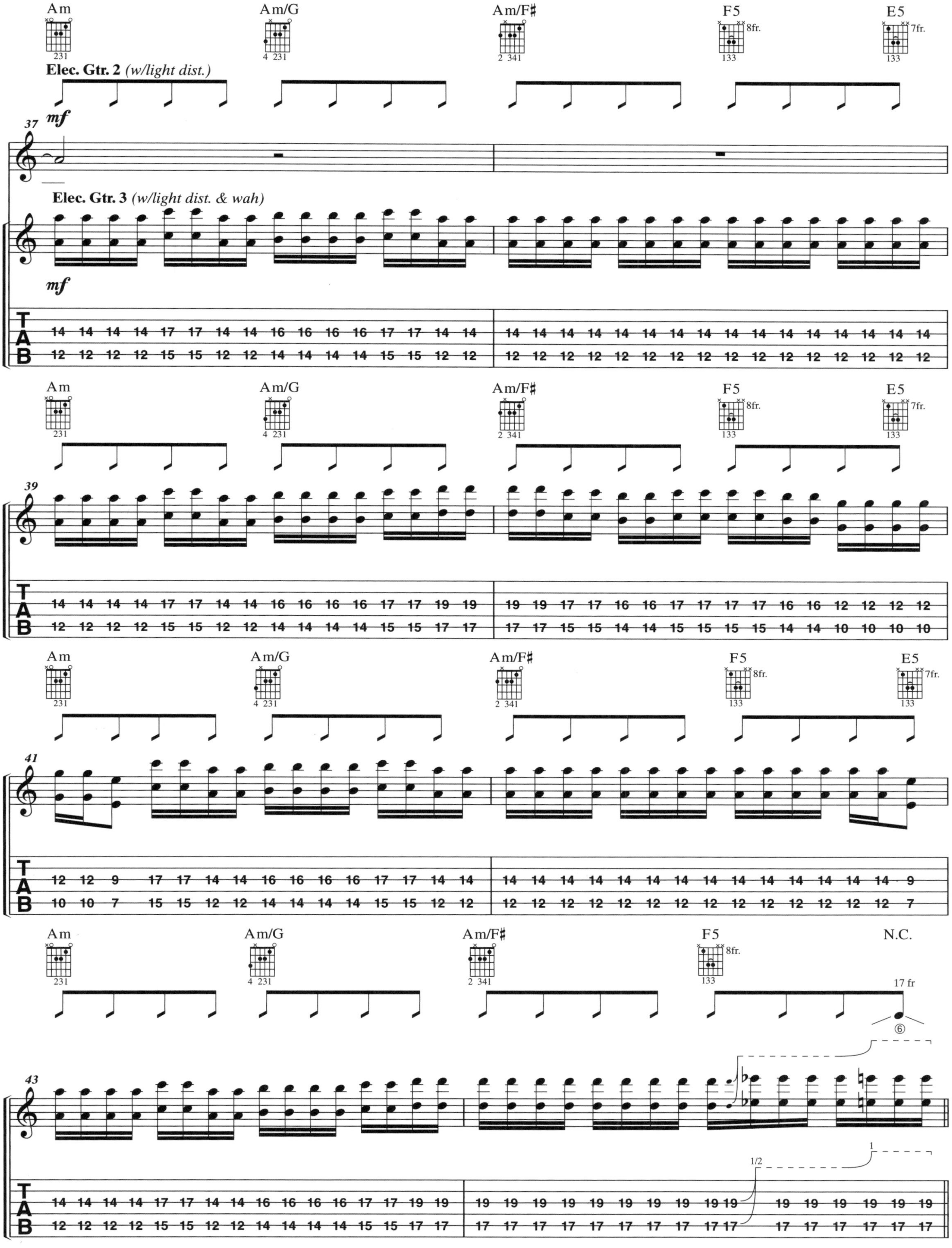

Am Am/G Am/F♯ F5 8fr. E5 7fr.

Elec. Gtr. 2 *(w/light dist.)*

37 *mf*

Elec. Gtr. 3 *(w/light dist. & wah)*

mf

Am Am/G Am/F♯ F5 8fr. E5 7fr.

39

Am Am/G Am/F♯ F5 8fr. E5 7fr.

41

Am Am/G Am/F♯ F5 8fr. N.C.

17 fr

43

1/2 1

Chorus:
Am
Am/G
F#m7(b5)
D5
Elec. Gtr. 2
I'm e - lat - ed,
med - i - cat - ed.
I am my own worst en - e - my.
G5
E
12 fr
So what ails you
s'what im - pales you.
You are your own worst en - e - my.
You're a vic - tim
of the sys - tem.
You're a vic - tim
of the sys - tem.
You are your own worst en - e - my.
Outro:
A5
F5
E5
Elec. Gtr. 3
T
A
B

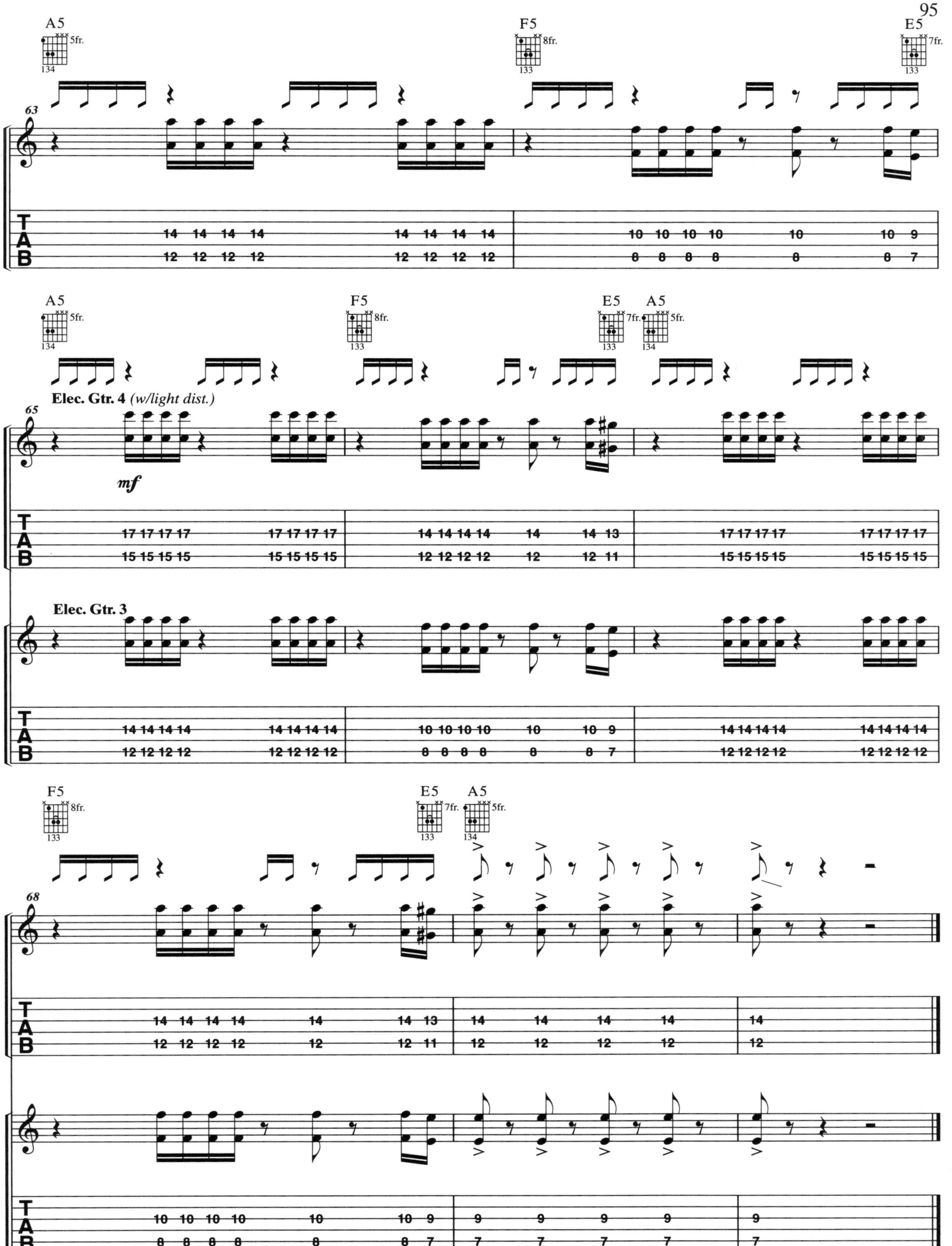
A5
F5
E5
Elec. Gtr. 4 (w/light dist.)
mf
Elec. Gtr. 3

HORSESHOES AND HANDGRENADES

Lyrics by BILLIE JOE
Music by GREEN DAY

A5 F♯5 A5 B5 D5 E5 A5 F♯5

B5 D5 E5 A5 F♯5 A5 B5 D5 E5 A5 F♯5 A5

Rhy. Fig. 1

Elec. Gtrs. 1 & 2

end Rhy. Fig. 1

*B5 Asus E/G♯ G5

1. I'm not fuck-ing a-round._

Elec. Gtr. 1

Elec. Gtr. 2

*Chords are implied (meas. 14–17)

Verses 1 & 2:

w/Rhy. Fig. 1 *(Elec. Gtrs. 1 & 2) 4 times, simile*

18 B5 D5 E5 A5 F♯5 A5 B5 D5 E5

I think I'm com - ing out.
I'm gon - na rip it out.

21 A5 F♯5 A5 B5 D5 E5 A5 F♯5 A5

All the de - ceiv - ers and cheat - ers, I think we've got a bleed - er right now.
Well, ev - 'ry - thing that you em - ploy was meant for me to de - stroy to the ground

24 B5 D5 E5 A5 F♯5 A5 B5 D5 E5

now.
Want you to slap me a - round.
So don't you fuck me a - round

27 A5 F♯5 A5 B5 D5 E5 A5 F♯5 A5

Want you to knock me out. Well, you
be - cause I'll shoot you down. I'm gon - na

30 B5 D5 E5 A5 F♯5 A5

missed me, kissed me, now you bet - ter kick me down.
drink, fight and fuck and I'm push - ing my luck all the time

32 B5 D5 E5 A5 F♯5 A5

now.

Chorus:

34 E A5 B

May - be you're the run - ner - up, but the first one to lose the race.

Elec. Gtrs. 1 & 2

A5 5fr. 134 — E 7fr. 1333

37

Al-most on - ly real - ly counts in horse-

F♯5 134

40

1. 2.

- shoes and hand gre - nades. 2.I'm gon - na burn it all down.

Bridge 1:

B5 7fr. 134 — A5 5fr. 134 — B5 7fr. 134 — A5 5fr. 134

43

De - mo - li - tion, self de - struc - tion,

Elec. Gtrs. 1 & 2

B5 7fr. 134 — A5 5fr. 134 — B5 7fr. 134 — A5 5fr. 134 — N.C.

45

what to an - ni - hi - late, this age - old con - tra - dic - tion.

Interlude:
w/Rhy. Fig. 1 (Elec. Gtrs. 1 & 2) 2 times, simile
Cont. ad lib. vocal
B5 D5 E5 A5 F♯5 A5 B5 D5 E5 A5 F♯5 A5
Instrumental:
*B5 Asus E/G♯ G5
Elec. Gtr. 1
Elec. Gtr. 2
*Chords are implied (meas. 55–62)
B5 Asus E/G♯ G5

Bridge 2:

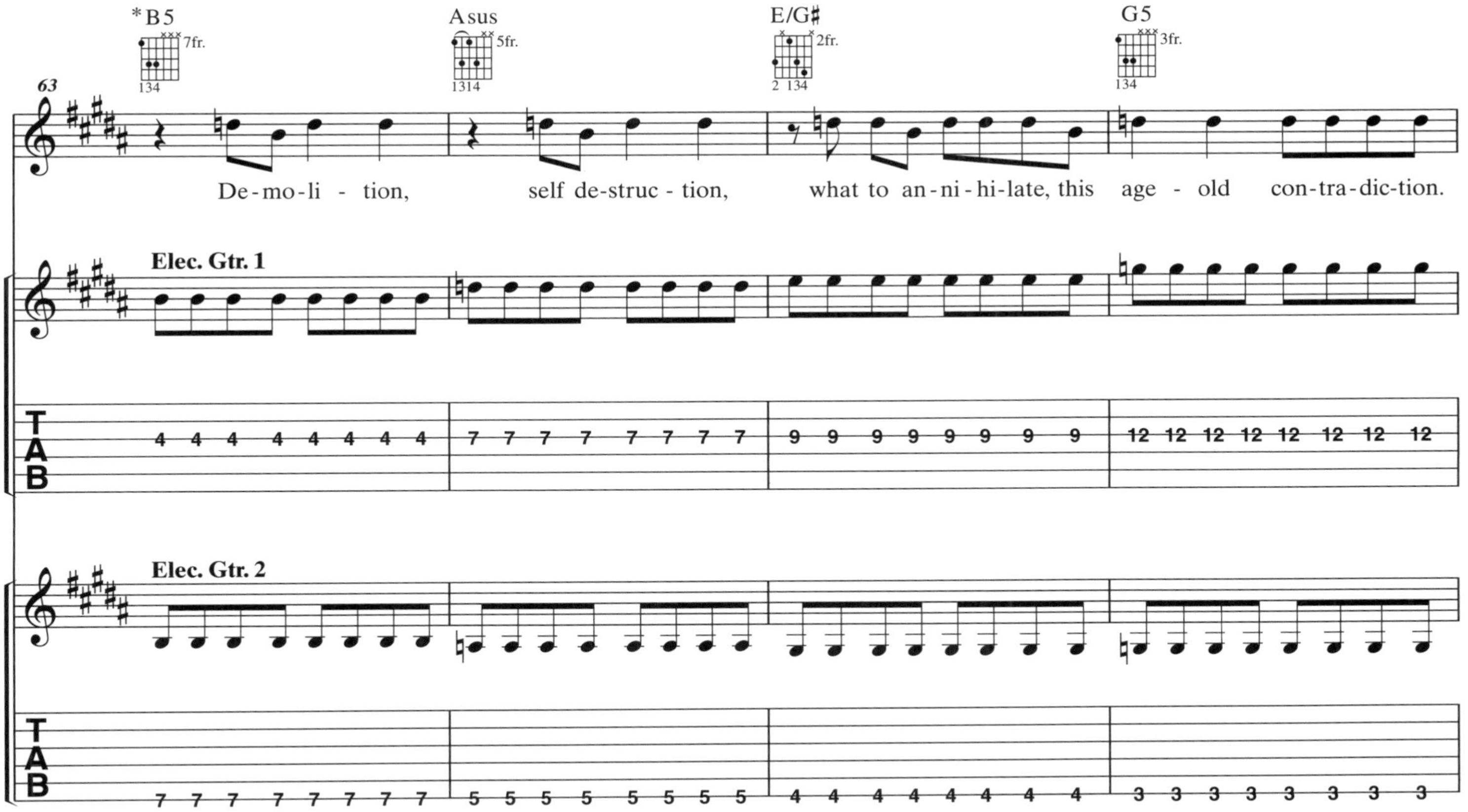
*B5
7fr.
134
Asus
5fr.
1314
E/G♯
2fr.
2 134
G5
3fr.
134
63
De-mo-li - tion, self de-struc - tion, what to an-ni-hi-late, this age - old con-tra-dic-tion.
Elec. Gtr. 1
T
A
B
4 4 4 4 4 4 4 4
7 7 7 7 7 7 7 7
9 9 9 9 9 9 9 9
12 12 12 12 12 12 12 12
Elec. Gtr. 2
T
A
B
7 7 7 7 7 7 7 7
5 5 5 5 5 5 5 5
4 4 4 4 4 4 4 4
3 3 3 3 3 3 3 3

*Chords are implied (meas. 63–70)

B5
7fr.
134
Asus
5fr.
1314
E/G♯
2fr.
2 134
G5
3fr.
134
67
De-mo-li - tion, self de-struc - tion, what to an-ni-hi-late, this old age.
T
A
B
4 4 4 4 4 4 4 4
7 7 7 7 7 7 7 7
9 9 9 9 9 9 9 9
12 12 12
T
A
B
7 7 7 7 7 7 7 7
5 5 5 5 5 5 5 5
4 4 4 4 4 4 4 4
3 3 3

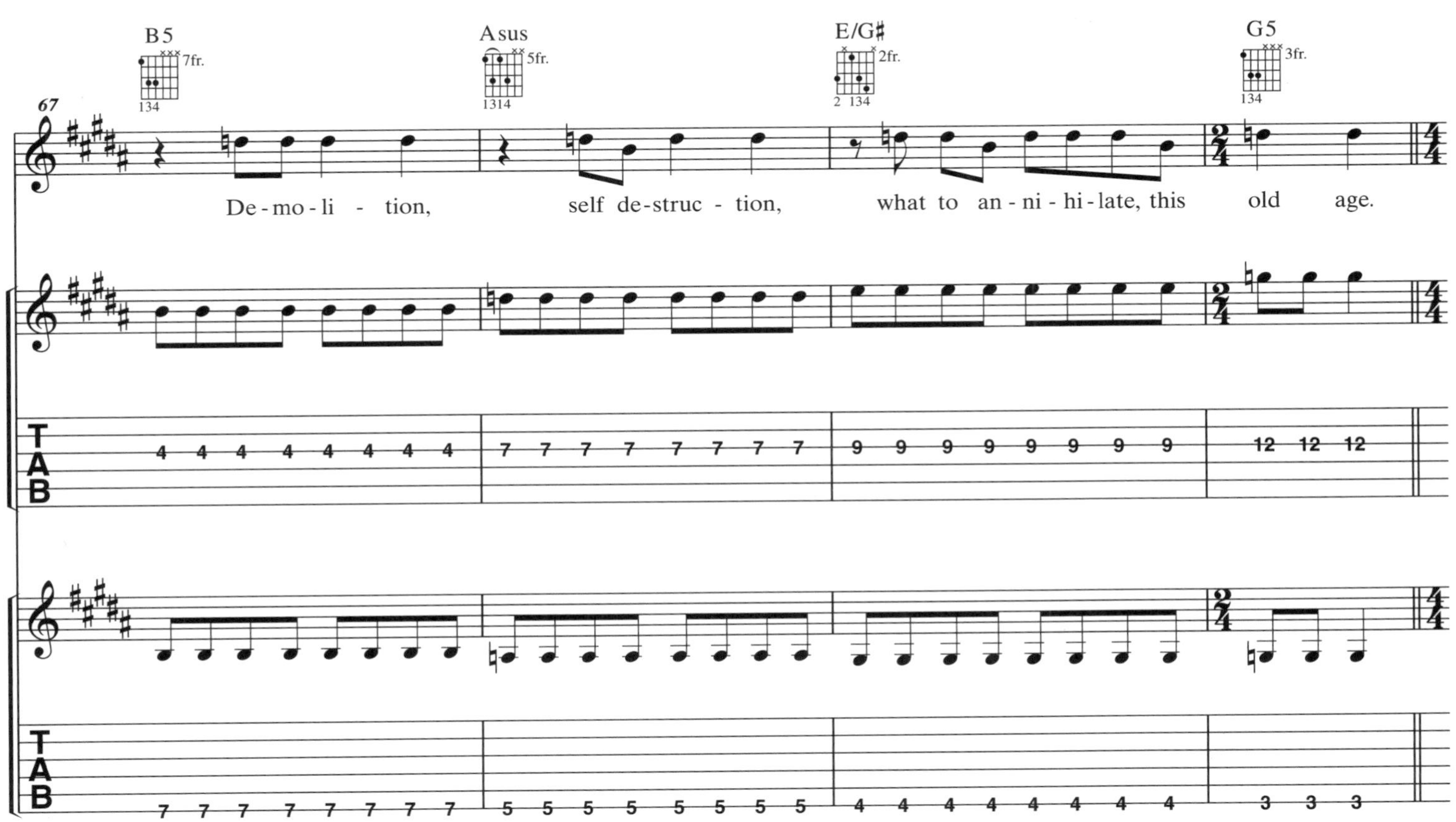

Interlude:
Band tacet
B5
D5
E5
A5
F♯5
A5
7fr.
5fr.
134
133
Elec. Gtr. 1
B5
D5
E5
A5
F♯5
N.C.
I'm not f*** - ing a - round.
Verse 3:
w/Rhy. Fig. 1 (Elec. Gtrs. 1 & 2) 2 times, simile
I think I'm com - ing out.
Well, I'm a hat - er, a trai - tor in a pair - of Chuck Tay - lors right now.
I'm not fuck - ing a - round.

B5
D5
E5
A5
7fr.
5fr.
134
133
83
86
89
Elec. Gtrs. 1 & 2
G - L - O - R - I - A!
G - L - O - R - I - A!
G - L - O - R - I - A!
G - L - O - R - I - A!
G - L - O - R - I - A!

THE STATIC AGE

w/Rhy. Fig. 1 (Elec. Gtr. 1) 1st 7 meas. only
E
F#
B
noid,__ mu - sic to my ner - vous sys - tem. Ad - ver - tis - ing
crete,__ Co - ca Co - la ex - e - cu - tion. Con - science on a
love and re - li gion,__ mur - der on the air - waves.
cross and your heart's in a vice,__ squeez - ing out your state of mind;
Slo - gans on the brink of cor - rup tion,__ vi - sions of__
are__ what you own that you can - not buy?__ What a fuck - ing
F#5
blas - phe-my, war and peace, oh,__ scream - ing__ at you.
trag - e - dy, strat - e - gy, oh,__ scream - ing__ at you.
Elec. Gtr. 1
Elec. Gtr. 2 (w/dist.)
P.M.
Cont. in slashes
Chorus:
Elec. Gtrs. 1 & 2
I can't see a thing in the vid - e - o. I can't hear a sound on the ra - di - o

B E F♯ B
1.
F♯
in ste-re-o in the__ stat - ic__ age.______
w/Rhy. Fig. 1 (Elec. Gtr. 1)
*B E F♯
*Chords are implied. Elec. Gtr. 2 tacet.
B E F♯
D.S. 𝄋
2.
F♯ B E F♯
I can't see a thing in the vid - e - o.
B E F♯ B
I can't hear a sound on the ra - di - o in ste - re - o
E F♯ B Bsus B
in the__ stat - ic__ age.______

Bridge:
E
7fr.
1333
B
7fr.
134211
Elec. Gtr. 2
57
Hey, hey, it's the stat - ic age. Well, this is how the west was won.
E
7fr.
1333
F♯
9fr.
F
8fr.
F♯
9fr.
G
10fr.
61
Hey, hey, it's the stat - ic age mil-len - ni - um.
Elec. Gtr. 3 (w/light dist.)
mf
T
A
B
15
Interlude:
C
3fr.
1333
F
134211
Elec. Gtr. 2
65
Elec. Gtr. 3
5 5 5 5 5 5 5 5
3 3 3 3 3 3 3 3
5 5 5 9 7 5
3 3 3 7 5 3
10 10 10 10 10 10 10
8 8 8 8 8 8 8
G
3fr.
134211
C
3fr.
1333
7 7 7 7 7 7 10 10
5 5 5 5 5 5 8 8
9 9 9 9 9 9 9 9
7 7 7 7 7 7 7 7
9 9 9 9 7 5
7 7 7 7 5 3

1.
2.
F
Fsus
F
G
Gsus
G
G
G♯
A
A♯
B
C
C♯
D
D♯
Verse 3:
D
G
A
Elec. Gtr. 1
All I want to know is a god - damned thing,_ not what's in the med - i - cine.
Elec. Gtr. 3
8va throughout
D
G
A
Cont. rhy. simile
All I want to do is I want to breathe,_ bat - ter - ies are not in - clud - ed.

D
G
A
85
What's the latest way that a man can die, screaming Hallelujah?
89
Singing out "the dawn's early light." The silence of the
Asus
Elec. Gtr. 1
92
rotten, forgotten, oh, screaming at you.
Elec. Gtr. 2
P.M.
Cont. in slashes

Chorus:

D
G
A
5fr.
3fr.
1333
134211
Elec. Gtrs. 1 & 2
96
I can't see a thing in the vid-e-o. I can't hear a sound on the ra-di-o
100
in ste-re-o in the_ stat - ic_ age._
1.
2.
105
I can't see a thing in the vid-e-o. I can't hear a sound on the ra-di-o
Whoa._ Whoa._
109
in ste-re-o in the_ stat - ic_ age,_
113
B♭
C
the stat - ic age._

21 GUNS

Lyrics by BILLE JOE
Music by GREEN DAY

Moderately slow ♩ = 84

Intro:

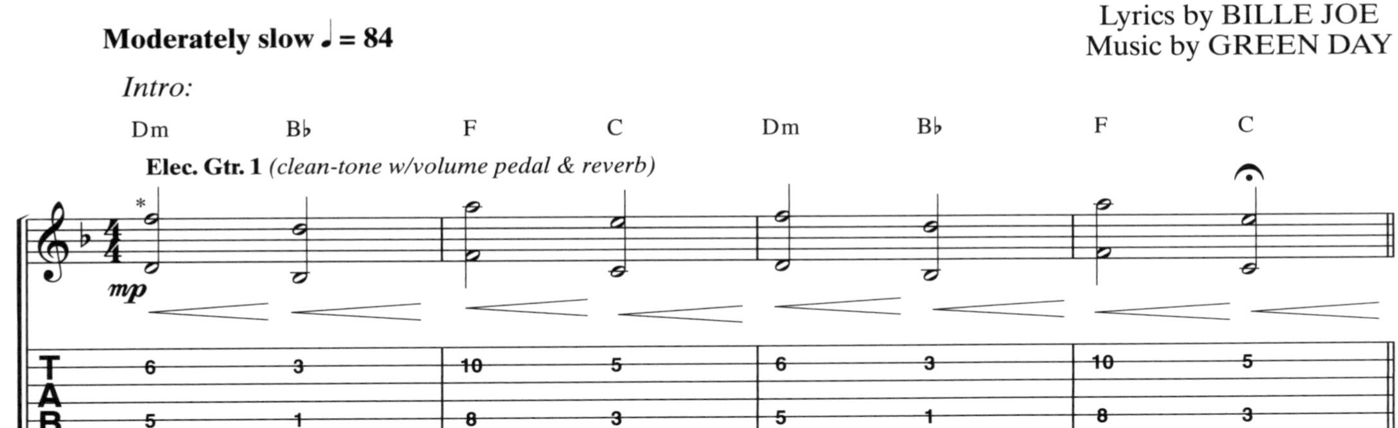

*To simulate volume pedal effect: With volume turned down on guitar, hammer both notes with left hand while gradually turning up the volume knob on the guitar to create bowed effect, then gradually turn volume down. Repeat for each note group.

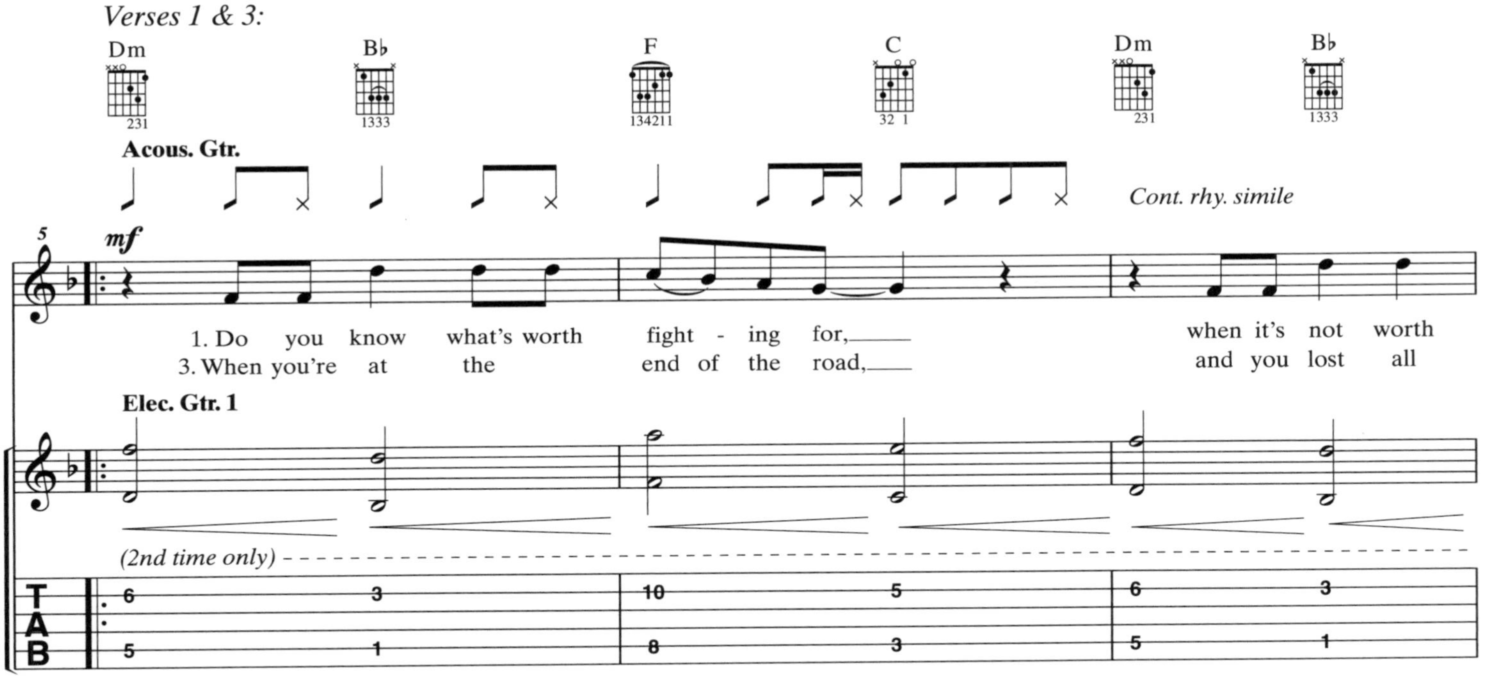

Verses 1 & 3:

Dm Bb F C Dm Bb

Acous. Gtr. *Cont. rhy. simile*

5 *mf*

1. Do you know what's worth fighting for, when it's not worth
3. When you're at the end of the road, and you lost all

Elec. Gtr. 1

(2nd time only)

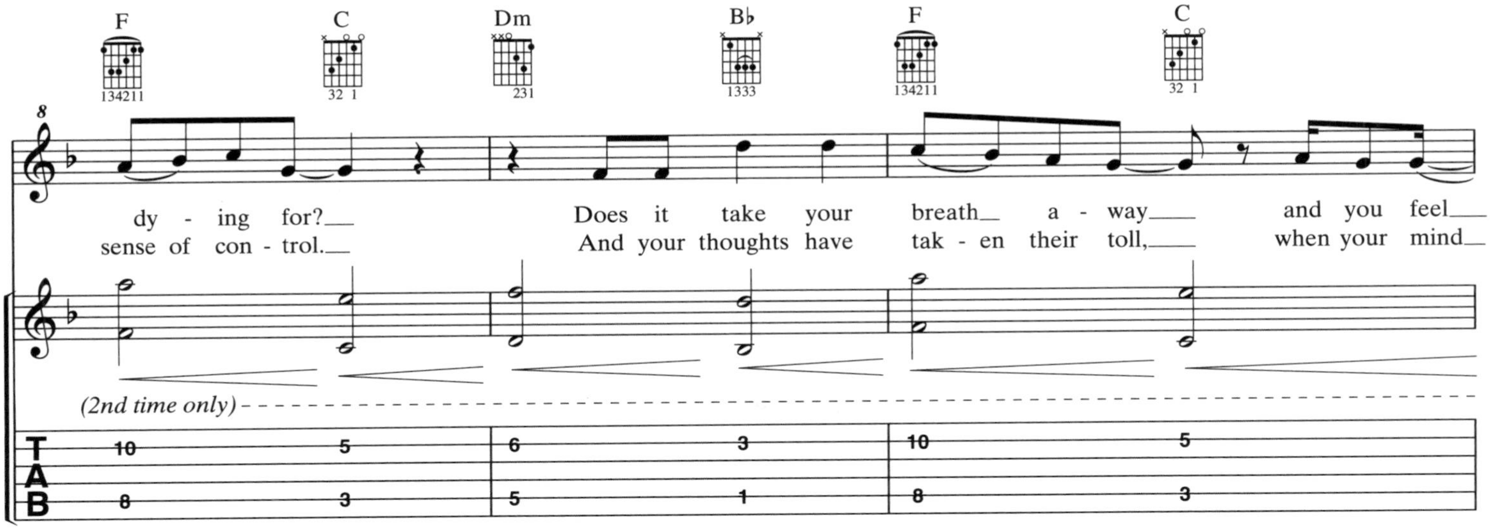

F C Dm Bb F C

8

dy - ing for? Does it take your breath a - way and you feel
sense of con - trol. And your thoughts have tak - en their toll, when your mind

(2nd time only)

Band enters
Verses 2 & 4:
B♭
C
Dm
B♭
Acous. Gtr. cont. rhy. simile
your - self suf - fo - cat - ing?
breaks the spir - it of your soul.
2. Does the pain weigh
4. Your faith walks on
(2nd time only)
(both times)
F
C
Dm
B♭
F
C
out the pride?
bro - ken glass,
And you look for a place to hide?
and the hang - o - ver does - n't pass.
(both times)
Dm
B♭
F
C
B♭
C
Acous. Gtr.
Did some-one break your heart in - side, you're in ru - ins.
Noth - ing's ev - er built to last, you're in ru - ins.
Elec. Gtr. 2
(w/light dist.)
mf
(both times)

Chorus:
Dm
C
Dm
C
B♭
F
Acous. Gtr.
One, twen - ty one guns, lay down your arms, give up the fight.
(Ah.
Elec. Gtr. 2
C
3fr.
Dm
C
Dm
C
One, twen - ty - one guns, throw up your arms
)
Elec. Gtr. 3 (w/light dist.)
mf

B♭
1333
F
134211
C
3fr.
1333
27
in - to the sky,
you and I.
(Ah.
)
(Ah.
3/5 6 8
1.
2.
30
)
)
20

Bridge:
Dm
5fr.
134211
B♭
6fr.
134211
F
134211
C
3fr.
1333
Dm
5fr.
134211
B♭
6fr.
134211
Acous. Gtr.
32
Did you try to___ live on your own, when you burned down the
Elec. Gtr. 4 (w/light dist.)
mf
Elec. Gtr. 2
F
134211
A
5fr.
134211
Dm
5fr.
134211
B♭
6fr.
134211
F
134211
A
5fr.
134211
35
house and home?___ Did you stand too___ close to the fi - re? Like a li -

B♭
1333
C
3fr.
1333
38
- ar look - ing for for - give - ness from a stone.
Guitar Solo:
F
134211
C
32 1
Dm
231
C
32 1
B♭
1333
F
134211
C
3fr.
1333
Acous. Gtr.
Cont. rhy. simile
40
Elec. Gtr. 4
Elec. Gtr. 2

F
C
Dm
C
B♭
F
44
C
3fr.
B♭
F
A
5fr.
Elec. Gtr. 5 (w/light dist.)
mf
47
Band tacet
Interlude:
Dm
B♭
F
C
Dm
B♭
F
C
Elec. Gtr. 1
50
Band cont. tacet
Verse 5:
Dm
B♭
F
C
Dm
B♭
F
C
Acous. Gtr.
54
When it's time to live and let die,
and you can't get an - oth - er try.

Dm
B♭
F
C
B♭
Some - thing in - side this heart has died, you're in ru - ins.
Elec. Gtr. 1
Band re-enters
Chorus:
F
C
Dm
C
B♭
F
Elec. Gtr. 2 & Acous. Gtr. resume chorus fig. simile
One, twen - ty - one guns, lay down your arms, give up the fight.
(Ah.
C
F
C
Dm
C
One, twen - ty - one guns, throw up your arms
)
Elec. Gtr. 3
B♭
F
C
F
C
in - to the sky.
One, twen - ty - one guns,
(Ah.
)

Dm
C
B♭
F
C
3fr.
lay down your arms, give up the fight.
(Ah.)
F
C
Dm
C
B♭
F
One, twen - ty - one guns, throw up your arms into the sky,
(Ah.
C
B♭
F
C
Acous. Gtr.
you and I.
)
(Ah.)
Elec. Gtr. 2

AMERICAN EULOGY

(A. Mass Hysteria - B. Modern World)

Lyrics by BILLIE JOE
Music by GREEN DAY

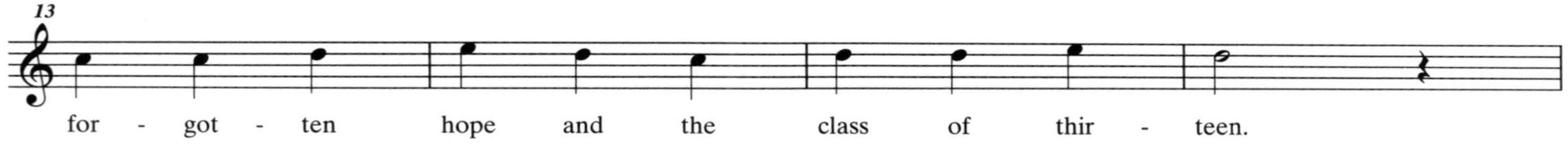

A. Mass Hysteria
Chorus:
C
D♭
A♭
3fr.
4fr.
1333
134211
te - ri - a. Mass hys - te - ri - a. Mass hys -
Rhy. Fig. 1
Elec. Gtr. 1 (w/light dist.)
mf
Rhy. Fig. 1A
Elec. Gtr. 2 (w/light dist.)
te - ri - a. Mass hys - te - ri - a.
end Rhy. Fig. 1
end Rhy. Fig. 1A

Verse:
D♭
A♭
G♭
4fr.
1333
134211
Elec. Gtr. 1
1. Red a - lert is the col - or of pan - ic, el - e - vat - ed to the point of stat - ic. Beat - ing in - to the hearts of the fa - nat - ics and the neigh - bor - hood's a load - ed gun.
2. True sounds of ma - ni - a - cal laugh - ter, and the deaf-mute's mis - lead - ing the cho - ir. The punch-line is a nat - u - ral dis - as - ter and it's sung by the un - em - ployed.
I - dle thought leads to full - throt - tle scream - ing, and the wel - fare's as - phyx - i - at - ing.
Fight fi - re with a ri - ot, the class war is hang - ing on a wi - re.
(Ooh.)
TAB

D♭
4fr.
1333
A♭
4fr.
134211
Mass con - fu - sion is all the new rage, and that's cre -
Be - cause the mar - tyr is a com - pul - sive li - ar when he
G♭
134211
A♭
4fr.
134211
at - ing a feed - ing ground for the bot - tom feed - ders.
said, "It's just a bunch of nig - gers throw - ing gas in - to the..."
Hys -
Chorus:
w/Rhy. Figs. 1 (Elec. Gtr. 1) & 1A (Elec. Gtr. 2)
C
3fr.
1333
D♭
4fr.
1333
A♭
4fr.
134211
te - ri - a. Mass hys - te - ri - a. Mass hys -
1.
2.
te - ri - a. Mass hys - te - ri - a.
Half-time feel / Band tacet 8 meas.
Bridge:
D♭
4fr.
1333
D♭/C
3fr.
1444
B♭m
13421
A♭
43111
There's a dis - tur - bance on the o - cean - side, they tapped in - to the re - serve.
Acous. Gtr.
mf
*On the recording Acous. Gtr. is tuned down 1/2 step and played with open chords in the key of D,
but for this arrangement, Acous. Gtr. was arranged to play in concert key to keep all guitars in standard tuning.

G♭
E♭m
A♭
the stat-ic re-sponse is so un - clear now.
Elec. Gtr. 1
D♭
D♭/C
B♭m
A♭
Acous. Gtr. cont. simile for 6 meas.
May-day, this is not a test! As the neigh - bor-hood burns,
Elec. Gtr. 1
End half-time feel
Acous. Gtr. tacet
G♭
E♭m
G
A♭
A - mer - i - ca is fall - ing. Vig - i -

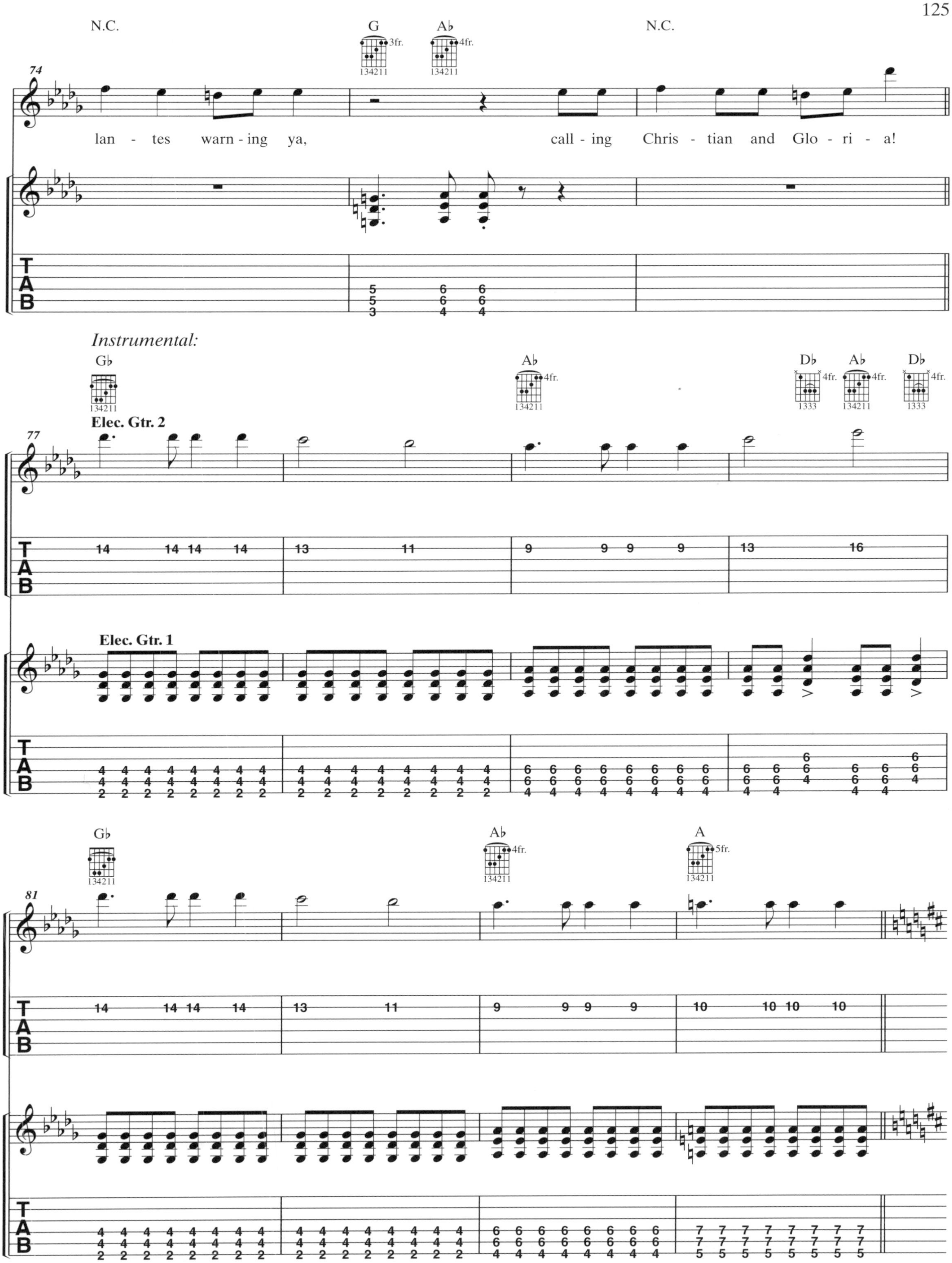

N.C. G A♭ N.C.

74

lan - tes warn - ing ya, call - ing Chris - tian and Glo - ri - a!

Instrumental:

G♭ A♭ D♭ A♭ D♭

77

Elec. Gtr. 2

Elec. Gtr. 1

G♭ A♭ A

81

D
A
G
A
G
A
D
A
G
A
N.C.
Elec. Gtr. 2
Elec. Gtr. 3 (w/light dist.)
mf
Elec. Gtr. 1
B. Modern World
Chorus:
I don't want to live in the mod - ern world,
I don't want to live in the mod - ern world.
I don't want to live in the mod - ern world,
I don't want to live in the mod - ern world. Well, I'm the

Verse 1:
D A G D A
class of thir - teen in the er - a of dis - sent. A hos - tage of the soul on a
G A D A G D
strike to pay the rent. The last of the reb - els with - out a com - mon ground. I'm
Chorus:
A G A D N.C. D A
gon - na light a fi - re in - to the un - der - ground. Well... I don't want to live in the
G A D A G A
mod - ern world, I don't want to live in the mod - ern world.

D A G A D A G A
I don't want to live in the mod - ern world, I don't want to live in the mod - ern world.
Bridge:
Bm F#5 G D
I am a na - tion with - out bu - reau - crat - ic ties.
A/C# Bm F#5
De - ny the al - le - ga - tion as
G A
it's writ - ten, f*** - ing lies.

Guitar Solo:
D
A
G
A
5fr.
3fr.
1333
134211
122
Elec. Gtr. 2
Elec. Gtr. 1
126
N.C.
Well, I

*Chords implied by bass gtr.

Band tacet
N.C.
D
A
G
D
5fr.
3fr.
1333
134211
142
mon - ey to burn on a min - i - mum_wage, well, I don't give a shit a - bout the mod - ern age. Yeah!
T
A
B
Chorus:
146
Elec. Gtr. 1 resume chorus fig. simile (see meas. 105–112)
I don't want to live in the mod - ern world, I don't want to live in the mod - ern world.
150
I don't want to live in the mod - ern world, I don't want to live in the mod - ern world.
Mass hys -
154
Elec. Gtr. 1 cont. simile
I don't want to live in the mod - ern world, I don't want to live in the mod - ern world.
te - ri - a. Mass hys - te - ri - a. Mass hys -
Repeat and fade
158
I don't want to live in the mod - ern world, I don't want to live in the mod - ern world.
te - ri - a. Mass hys - te - ri - a. Mass hys -

SEE THE LIGHT

Lyrics by BILLIE JOE
Music by GREEN DAY

D♭ A♭ D♭ A♭

non - be - liev - ers go be - yond be - lief. Then I

* Tremolo pick in a 16th-note pattern while sliding left-hand finger down string.

Chorus:
G♭
D♭
A♭
4fr.
134211
1333
I just want to see the light.
And I,
hold throughout
I don't want to lose my sight.
Well, I,

G♭
D♭
A♭
D♭
A♭
D♭
28
I just want to see the light.
And I
G♭
D♭
E♭
A♭
E♭
A♭
C
32
need to know what's worth the fight.

𝄋 *Verses 2 & 3:*

w/Rhy. Fig. 2 *(Elec. Gtr. 2) 3 times*
w/Rhy. Figs. 1 *(Piano)* **& 1A** *(Elec. Gtr. 1), both 8 times, simile*

36
Db Ab Db Ab
2. I've been wast - ed, pills and al - co - hol, and
(3.) crossed the des - ert, reach - ing high - er ground, then I

40
Db Ab Db Ab
I've been chas - ing down the pool halls. Then I
pound the pave - ment to take the li - ars down. But it's

44
Db Ab Db Ab
drank the wa - ter from a hur - ri - cane, and I
gone for - ev - er, but nev - er too late, where the

48
Db Ab Db Ab **w/Fill 1** *(Elec. Gtr. 3)* Db
set a fi - re just to see the flame.
ev - er af - ter is in the hands of fate.
Well, I,

Elec. Gtr. 2

Chorus:

Elec. Gtrs. 1 & 2 resume chorus fig. simile (see meas. 20–33)

52
Gb Db Ab Db Ab Db
I just want to see the light. And I,

56
Gb Db Ab Db Ab Db
I don't want to lose my sight. Well, I,

Gb
Db
Ab
4fr.
134211
1333
60
I just want to see the light. And I
To Coda
Band tacet
w/Fill 1 (Elec. Gtr. 3)
Eb
N.C.
6fr.
64
need to know what's worth the fight.
Elec. Gtr. 4 (w/light dist.)
mf
Guitar Solo:
Elec. Gtr. 2 resume chorus fig. simile (see meas. 20–35)
68
72
76

Gb
Db
Eb
Ab
C
4fr.
6fr.
3fr.
134211
1333
D.S. 𝄋 al Coda
3. Well, I
Elec. Gtr. 2
Coda
what's worth the fight.
Elec. Gtr. 1

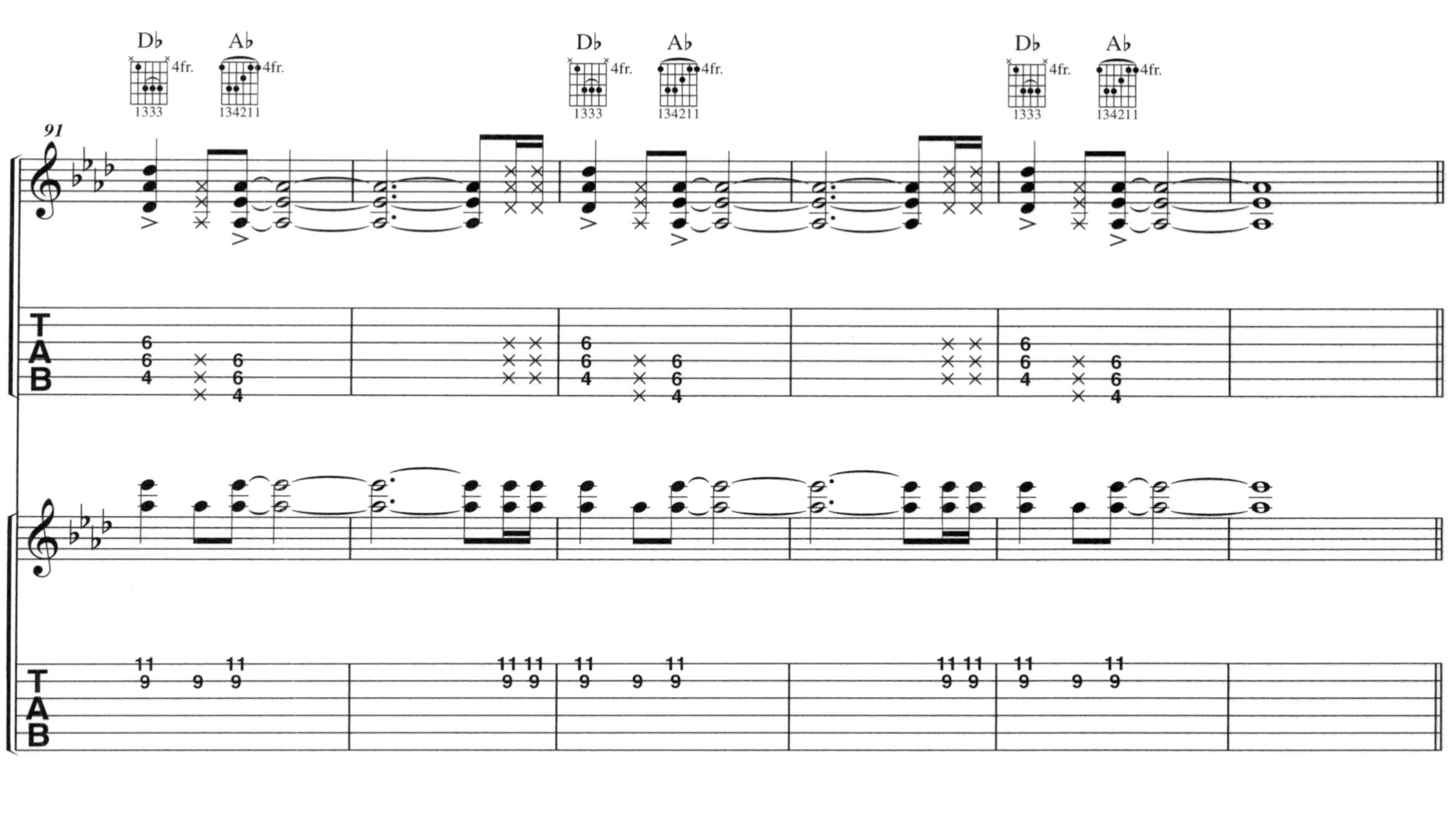

Outro:

Repeat and fade

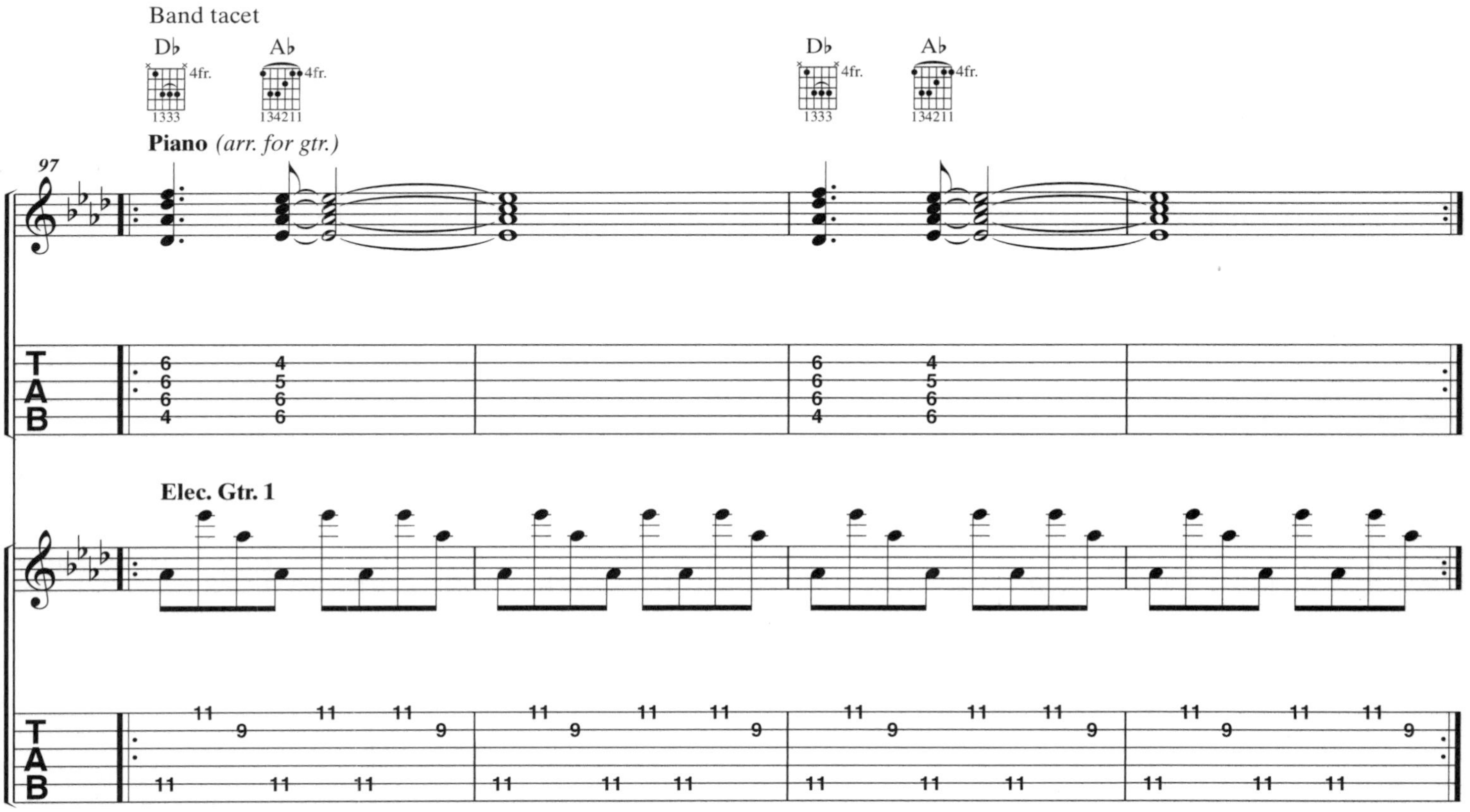

Band tacet

D♭ 4fr. 1333 A♭ 4fr. 134211 D♭ 4fr. 1333 A♭ 4fr. 134211

97

Piano *(arr. for gtr.)*

Elec. Gtr. 1

GUITAR **TAB** GLOSSARY

TABLATURE EXPLANATION

TAB illustrates the six strings of the guitar.
Notes and chords are indicated by the placement of fret numbers on each string.

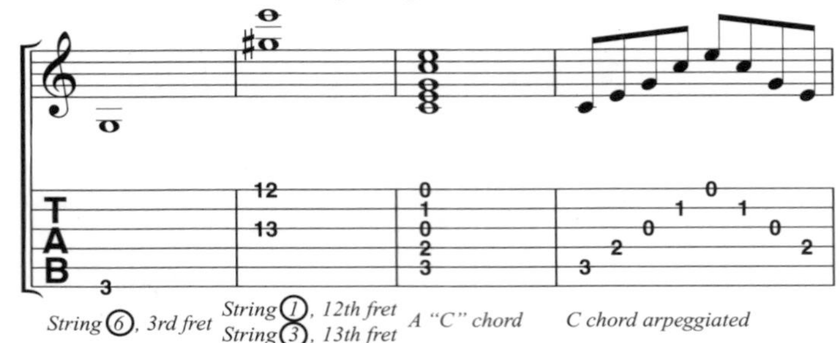

BENDING NOTES

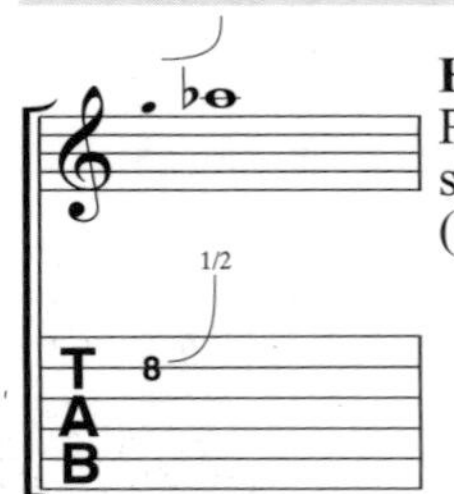

Half Step: Play the note and bend string one half step (one fret).

Whole Step: Play the note and bend string one whole step (two frets).

Slight Bend/ Quarter-Tone Bend: Play the note and bend string sharp.

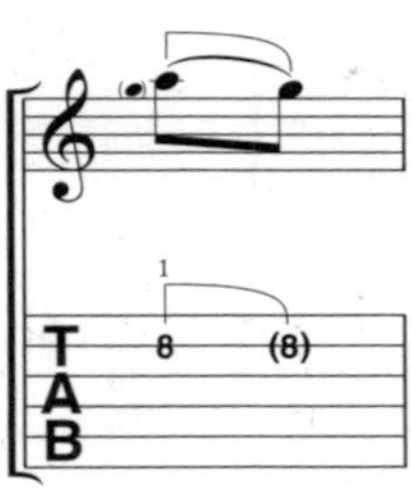

Prebend and Release: Play the already-bent string, then immediately drop it down to the fretted note.

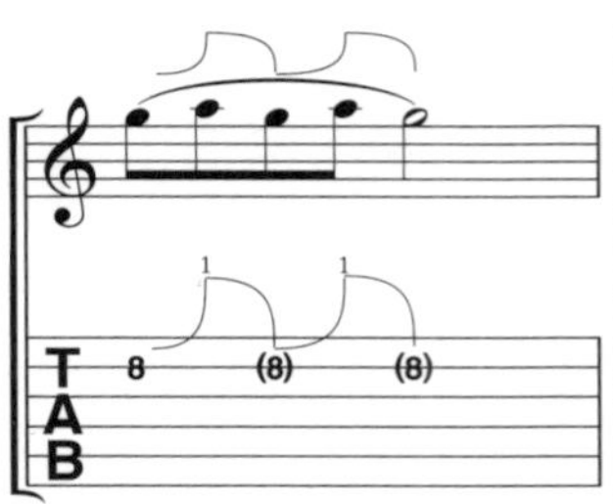

Bend and Release: Play the note and bend to the next pitch, then release to the original note. Only the first note is attacked.

PICK DIRECTION

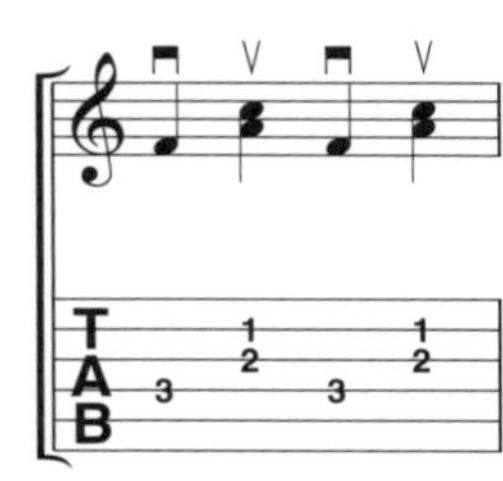

Downstrokes and Upstrokes: The downstroke is indicated with this symbol (⊓) and the upstroke is indicated with this (V).

ARTICULATIONS

Hammer On: Play the lower note, then "hammer" your finger to the higher note. Only the first note is plucked.

Pull Off: Play the higher note with your first finger already in position on the lower note. Pull your finger off the first note with a strong downward motion that plucks the string—sounding the lower note.

Palm Mute: The notes are muted (muffled) by placing the palm of the pick hand lightly on the strings, just in front of the bridge.

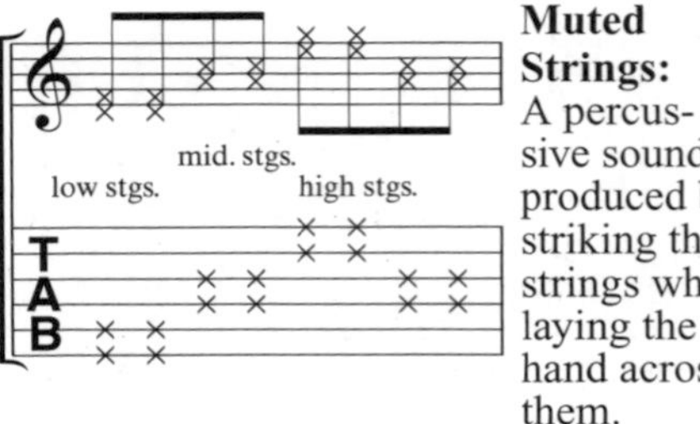

Muted Strings: A percussive sound is produced by striking the strings while laying the fret hand across them.

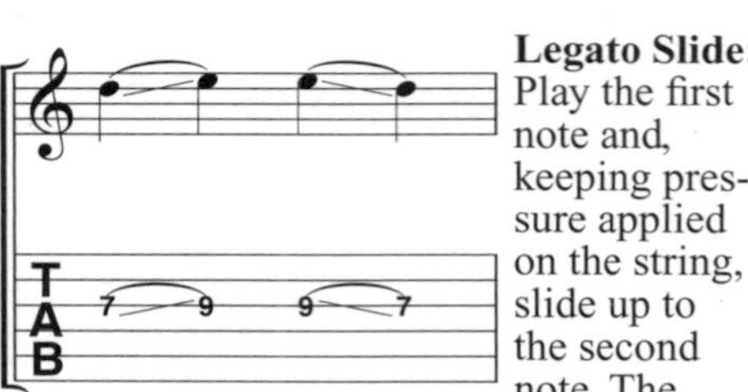

Legato Slide: Play the first note and, keeping pressure applied on the string, slide up to the second note. The diagonal line shows that it is a slide and not a hammer-on or a pull-off.

HARMONICS

Natural Harmonic: A finger of the fret hand lightly touches the string at the note indicated in the TAB and is plucked by the pick producing a bell-like sound called a harmonic.

Artificial Harmonic: Fret the note at the first TAB number, lightly touch the string at the fret indicated in parens (usually 12 frets higher than the fretted note), then pluck the string with an available finger or your pick.

RHYTHM SLASHES

Strum Marks/ Rhythm Slashes: Strum with the indicated rhythm pattern. Strum marks can be located above the staff or within the staff.

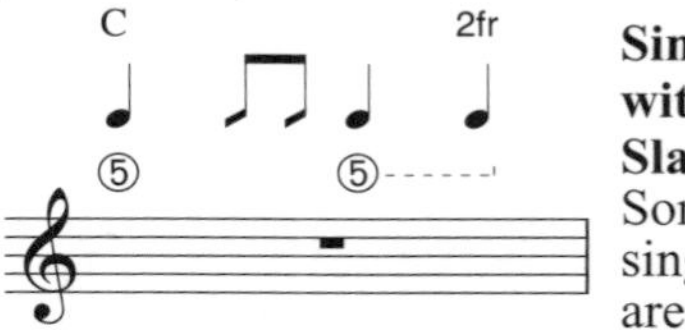

Single Notes with Rhythm Slashes: Sometimes single notes are incorporated into a strum pattern. The circled number below is the string and the fret number is above.